Illustrations © Jessica Hagy

Design by Alex Miles Younger

The Domino Project

Published by Do You Zoom, Inc.

The Domino Project is powered by Amazon. Sign up for updates and free stuff at www.thedominoproject.com.

This is the first edition. If you'd like to suggest a riff for a future edition, please visit our website.

End Malaria: Bold innovation, limitless generosity, and the opportunity to save a life / Editor: Michael Bungay Stanier

p. cm.

ISBN 978-1-936719-28-0

Printed in the United States of America

# END MALARIA

## BOLD INNOVATION, LIMITLESS GENEROSITY, AND THE OPPORTUNITY TO SAVE A LIFE

### 62 BUSINESS THINKERS PUSHING YOU TO RETHINK THE WAY YOU WORK

THE
DOMINO
PROJECT
POWERED BY amazon.com

# FOREWORD

Propped up on my desk is a small poster that's served as a useful reminder as we've put this project together. It's says:

*Don't undertake a project unless it is manifestly important and nearly impossible.*

Something is different because you've bought this book—mosquito nets are going to Africa. That means for every book you buy, we get that much closer to our goal of ending malaria.

More than fifty extraordinary writers and thinkers have come together to contribute to this project and to write about what they think is most important to let Great Work flourish in your life and your organization. Great Work is the work you do that has meaning and that you care about and that has an impact—in short, the work that matters.

The essays are organized into three major categories—Focus, Courage, and Resilience—and then eight additional subcategories.

Whether you follow Danielle LaPorte's suggestions on the value of obsession, Brené Brown's ideas on the power of vulnerability, or Josh Linkner's thoughts on an idea schedule (or any of the hundreds of other good ideas that are here), I challenge you to pick one or two ... or three ... and act on them. Because that's what this book is really about: taking action.

With $20 from each book going toward the eradication of malaria in Africa, we hope you'll be proud to share this book and campaign with the world. To learn how you can spread this message, visit EndMalariaDay.com.

*Michael Bungay Stanier, on behalf of The Domino Project, Malaria No More, and the many people who have contributed to the success of this book,* End Malaria.

## THE BUSINESS CASE FOR ENDING MALARIA

*End Malaria* will strike some as an odd title for a business book. But the number-one lesson in storytelling? Never bury the lead. The purpose of this compilation is to raise funds for the fight against malaria—a preventable and treatable disease that is spread by mosquitoes and kills more than 750,000 people every year. *End Malaria* puts the charitable mission of this project at center stage.

This book is a great example of how doing good makes good business sense. By purchasing *End Malaria*, you've donated $20 to Malaria No More to support our efforts to stop children from dying from the absurdity of a mosquito bite. But you've also given yourself the chance to learn from some of the biggest business greats in their respective industries, including Seth Godin, Alan Webber, Dan Pink, and Gina Trapani. Not a bad payout for helping families in Africa protect their children from a deadly disease.

Our approach to ending malaria is based on the same principles of any business. It starts with an idea and grows from there, taking one single spark of inspiration and adding just enough focus, courage, and resilience to make that idea a reality. Every good business sets out to accomplish a specific, deliverable goal, and fighting malaria is no different—our goal is to end malaria deaths in Africa by 2015.

The authors of this compilation came together to share their lessons learned in the business world and to give advice on how to get the most out of an idea, team, or business. Their shared goal is not just to do good work—but also to do good. By participating in this book—either by contributing to it or by purchasing it—you're helping African families defeat malaria once and for all.

Thank you for helping to put malaria out of business.

*Timothy "Scott" Case—a technologist, entrepreneur, and inventor—is a Vice Chairman of Malaria No More. Scott was recently named CEO of the Startup America Partnership, where he'll drive American entrepreneurship to create jobs and sustain U.S. global leadership. Previously co-founder of Priceline.com, Scott also serves as Chairman of Network for Good.*

# CHAPTERS AND CONTRIBUTORS

## TAP YOUR STRENGTHS

Kevin Kelly, *What You Don't Have To Do*

Roger Martin, *Thin-slicing*

Pam Slim, *The Voice in Your Head*

Mitch Joel, *Personal Branding Is Not Optional*

Premal Shah, *The Keys to Kiva*

Jon Acuff, *Dream Backward To Move Forward*

Sir Ken Robinson, *Find Your Element*

Michael Bungay Stanier, *I'm Scarred*

## CREATE FREEDOM

Derek Sivers, *In a Perfect World...*

Barry Schwartz, *The Choices That Matter*

Jonah Lehrer, *Don't Pay Attention*

Danielle LaPorte, *What Creative Types Already Know About Productivity*

Steven Johnson, *Genius Is In the Margins of Your Attention*

Steph Corker Irwin, *Permission To Be Funny*

Josh Linkner, *What's Your Idea Schedule?*

Jeff Jarvis, *Beta-think*

COURAGE

## LOVE & BE KIND

Brené Brown, *The Strength of Vulnerability*

Gary Vaynerchuk, *The Best Marketing Strategy Ever*

Eileen McDargh, *Work Is a Four-Letter Word*

Lauryn Ballesteros, *Just Make It Up*

Sally Hogshead, *Here's to the Haters*

Scott Stratten, *Three Words from Ann Landers*

Tom Peters, *Pursuing Excellence*

## DISRUPT NORMAL

Nancy Duarte, *Don't Be the Bland Leading the Bland*

Ryan Vanderbilt, *Thinking Was Ruining My Life*

Bill Jensen, *The Biggest Distance in the World*

Nilofer Merchant, *Avoiding Suck-ness and Silence*

Rich Fernandez, *You the Operating System*

Nicholas Carr, *Build Bridges*

Seth Godin, *Heads or Tails?*

## TAKE SMALL STEPS

Chris Guillebeau, *Ordinary Courage*

Jonathan Fields, *Dancing with Uncertainty*

Robert Biswas-Diener, *Stop Complaining and Muster the Courage to Lead*

Alexandra Levit, *Change Your Career While at Work Today*

Chris Brogan, *Countdown to Escape Velocity*

Dave Ramsey, *"Indecisive Leader" Is an Oxymoron*

Josh Kaufman, *Create a Personal Master Plan*

## EMBRACE SYSTEMS

David Allen, *The Strategic Value of Clear Space*

Dan Pink, *What's the Matter with Millennials?*

Richard E. Lapchick, *Good Work: Hoops Triumps in Senegal*

Gopi Kallayil, *Flourishing Inside the Lion's Den*

Melissa Daimler, *Learning in the New World of Work*

Les McKeown, *The Power of the Mundane*

Scott Belsky, *Reconsider Your Approach to Organization*

## GET PHYSICAL

Gwen Bell, *Unplug*

Jim Kouzes & Barry Posner, *Credibility Is the Foundation of Leadership*

Sally Bonneywell, Kim Lafferty, & Sue Cruse, *How Can We "Do More, Feel Better, Live Longer"?*

David Rock, *Rewards, Threats, and What Truly Motivates People*

Keith Ferrazzi, *The 15-Minute Secret*

Daymond John, *Living the Brand*

Tony Schwartz, *The 90-Minute Plan*

## COLLABORATE

Lynda Gratton, *Riding with the Posse*

Gina Trapani, *Reflections*

Gary E. Knell, *Muppet Marketing*

Charlene Li, *The Importance of Failure*

Patrick Lencioni, *Making Virtual Teams Work*

Andy Smith, *Make a Difference with Design Thinking*

Alan Webber, *What Does It Take To Do Great Work?*

Ashley Sleep, *Hope to Dream*

**Illustrations by Jessica Hagy**

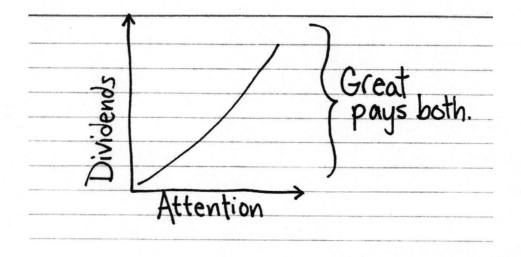

# FOCUS

*Malaria No More and its partners are working tirelessly to end malaria deaths in Africa by 2015.*

# TAP YOUR STRENGTHS

*"The magic is inside you. There ain't no crystal ball."*

Dolly Parton,
Music icon and philanthropist

If you live in a big city, you'll most likely have seen a skyscraper being built. It's an odd experience. It's not like there's steady progress from foundation to spire.

First, the builders dig a great big hole in the ground. And then, seemingly, they wait. Not much happens for months. But just as you begin to wonder if this project has been another victim of the economy, suddenly, like Spring blossoming, the building shoots up and is completed in a glass and steel flourish in no time. The secret lies in setting the foundations, making them deep, solid, and strong. In this first section, the contributors write about establishing your own foundation, focusing on what you're best at, and using that as the base for whatever it is that you're building.

## IN THIS SECTION

## WHAT YOU DON'T HAVE TO DO

When you start your first job, all your attention is focused on not screwing up. Your chief goal as a newbie is simply to do a good job. Working smart means doing what is required.

As you gain confidence in your ability to complete a job, your task is to learn new things, to take on additional chores. At this stage, working smart means doing more than is required.

The next level is exploration. As the number of additional tasks you try increases, you begin to see what you are good at (and not so good at). Working smart here means trying as many roles as you can in order to discover what you are best at.

As you educate yourself about your own talent and ambitions, you graduate from doing a task right to doing the right task. It takes some experience to realize that a lot of work is better left undone. It might be busywork that is performed out of habit, or it might be work that is heading in the wrong direction. Working smart means making sure you are spending your time on jobs that are effective and that actually need to be done.

But the smart journey doesn't end there. If you really pay attention to the feedback of those around you, and constantly strive to improve, you may eventually be able to discover your own best talents. At this stage, you can begin to do only the jobs that you are good at doing and that need to be done. And what a joy that is! For many years I thought this was the pinnacle of working wisdom. What could be more heavenly than to spend your energies only on those tasks you were both good at AND loved?

## KEVIN KELLY

*Kevin Kelly founded* Wired Magazine, *was its Executive Editor for many years, and remains its Senior Maverick. His most recent book is* What Technology Wants, *which follows the best-selling* New Rules for the New Economy. *Follow Kevin on the Web at kk.org and see him speak on TED.com.*

*Work at its smartest means doing that work that no one else can do.*

But recently it began to dawn on me that there is yet another stage beyond doing things well and with love.

It began with my experience as an editor of magazines. A large part of the editor's job is getting other people to complete stories based on ideas the editor (me) has. So I got used to handing over good ideas. But while I could assign most good ideas, every once in a while I'd get a great idea that I simply could not sell. I'd let it go, but a few of those left to die would be resurrected. So I would try again to give them away. Some got picked up, but a few would again get no assignment and retreat. A number of these ideas might go through this cycle a dozen times, until at the end I would have to face it: Here was an idea so good that I could not kill it, yet no one else wanted it.

It took me several times to realize that this was a signal. It said, "This is the one you have to do." These stories would become the best ones I ever wrote.

That's because these were the stories that no one else could write. What I had been inadvertently doing was weeding out good ideas that I could do (but others could do as well) from those few great ideas that only I could do. I had discovered that it was not enough to be able to do something well, and want to do it, and get paid for doing it. Work at its smartest means doing that work that no one else can do.

That's a pretty high bar. Becoming aware of what one can do well that others cannot is an immense challenge. In most cases, it takes our whole lives to discover this. This awareness arrives only through deliberate practice and with the help of others, but the payoff is equally immense. When you are doing something well that others want, and you are the only one who can do it, you will be uncommonly rewarded.

I think my experience may offer one useful tip in this process. When others are doing something similar to what you are, let that activity go because that means you don't have to do it! If people are stealing your ideas, ripping off your moves, or knocking off your style, and they are doing it well, thank them. You've just learned that this assignment is something you don't need to do because someone else can do it. This is scary because you are giving up things you do well, and you might think that after you surrender all the good stuff, there won't be anything excellent left for you. Trust me—there is more to you than that.

But it will take all your life to find it. All, as in all your days. And all, as in all your ceaseless effort. Your greatest job is shedding what you don't have to do.

## THIN-SLICING

The secret to making sure your work is as great as possible is to spend up-front time designing your work to involve the thinnest slice of you possible.

Our work is most fun and productive when we are doing only the work that we are the most qualified in the organization to do, and others around us are doing the work that they are the most qualified to do. Our work is least fun and productive when we are doing work that others around us are as or more qualified to do, but they aren't doing it because we have failed to design the work properly.

I think that generally, we take on too thick a slice of work tasks because often that is the way work is doled out. For example, the task of being Dean of the Rotman School of Management is doled out in one big bundle. If I actually did the bundle handed to me, I wouldn't be nearly as happy or productive as I am. The slice is so thick that I wouldn't be able to do the things that I am more qualified to do than those around me—such as writing articles and books that enhance the reputation of the School outside our home market.

In order to free up the time necessary to do those uniquely value-added things, I have had to design my job carefully to have other people do significant pieces of the thick slice doled out to me. For example, I had a very thick slice of budgeting, financial planning, and financial control. I also had a talented Chief Administrative Officer who had the capacity to grow into taking a significant part of the financial portfolio over from me. In my first two years as Dean, I spent disproportionate time redesigning the financial aspects of my job and that of the CAO, and I worked hard to make sure she and I were on the same page in terms of the School's financial strategy.

## ROGER MARTIN

*Roger Martin is the Dean of Rotman School of Management at the University of Toronto. He is the author of a number of books, including* The Design of Business *and* Fixing the Game. *Follow Roger on the Web at RogerLMartin.com.*

*Our work is most fun and productive when we are doing only the work that we are the most qualified in the organization to do, and others around us are doing the work that they are the most qualified to do.*

Thereafter, she ramped up her responsibilities dramatically, taking on new challenges that made her happier with her job, and freeing up many of my days. I did the same with the Vice-Dean, Academic, and the Vice-Dean, Programs, my Chief of Staff, and the heads of Marketing, Events, Advancement, and Alumni Affairs.

Together, these efforts had the effect of thinning my job down to the point that I could broaden it out dramatically. Many people ask whether I get any sleep when they look at the breadth of activities in which I engage. I answer that I love sleep and get plenty of it. They think otherwise because they imagine that I am taking a thick slice of everything I do. I don't; I relentlessly thin down.

One might wonder why everyone doesn't do the same thing. I believe the reason is that most people are unwilling to do the time-consuming design work up front. It is an investment—and a substantial one—in future personal productivity. If I had simply tossed a bunch of financial responsibilities to my CAO and wished her the best of luck, I don't think there would have been a happy ending. I had to work with her to make sure that she and I had a similar view of what we were trying to accomplish. I also had to work with my boss, the Provost of the University, to get permission to shift some of my responsibilities to my CAO. That work caused me to spend more of my time in my first year or two as Dean on the financial portfolio in my job than I would have spent had I just decided to keep the thick job. So there was a cost, a real cost. But I would argue that in the next decade, the savings have been easily ten times the up-front cost—and they are growing with each passing year.

But the key is that the CAO is happier—as are the others who have taken big slices of what could have and even should have been my job. And I am happier too!

## THE VOICE IN YOUR HEAD

I sat across the table from my smart and talented friend. He described his difficult path over the last year as he had fought to earn a healthy living from his creative gifts. He was already tremendously accomplished, with a solid corporate career. And he was in the middle of working on a big, important project outside of it.

"But," he said, "I am just not sure if I can really make this happen."

That kind of doubt, played out thousands of times a day in the minds of smart people, stops a lot of great work from happening.

You want to do something significant.

Like turn around a struggling division of your company.

Or start your business.

Or write your book.

So you read the best books, and learn from the best teachers. You are poised, ready to face the big challenge.

Except for one thing.

You can't quiet the voice in your head that says "Who am I to do this work?"

When you come to that moment of doubt—and you will—here are four ways to reclaim your authority.

## PAM SLIM

*Pam Slim is the author of* Escape from Cubicle Nation *and a champion for frustrated employees in corporate jobs who are breaking out and starting their own businesses. Follow Pam on Twitter at @PamSlim and on the Web at PamelaSlim.com, and watch her speak as part of the TEDx series.*

> *Without a deep root of meaning to anchor you, you will never survive the raging storm of what it takes to make great work happen.*

### Find your root

Your power does not come from a finite well of self-worth. It comes from a deeper place, from the part of your soul that understands that the work you do is not about you; it is about the people you affect with your work.

Ask a photographer why it is important to take two hundred shots to get one perfect frame. Ask a writer why it is worth revising an article until her shoulder is so tight that her arm goes numb on the keyboard. Ask a programmer why it is important to write smooth and elegant code and patiently work out bugs.

It is important because it creates a fantastic experience for the audience you care about.

Without a deep root of meaning to anchor you, you will never survive the raging storm of what it takes to make great work happen.

To find your root, answer the questions:

How do I want to affect the world?

Why is this important?

### Clarify your definition of success

A lot of people will tell you exactly what you need to do to be successful.

The problem is that there is no guarantee that their definition of success will make you happy. Not everyone wants to climb the career ladder or grow an intimate company into an empire. Some people don't want a white picket fence; they want to live looking out the window of an airplane.

Following someone else's vision of success will hold you back. If you have to ask for permission, you have already ceded authority.

To create your own definition of success, answer the questions:

What are the conditions that allow me to bring out my strengths, do my best work, and enjoy what I am doing while I do it?

How would my life look if I designed it to fit me perfectly?

## Assemble your crew

Doing great work can be lonely. The friends and colleagues who were happy to know you as one of the gang may not understand your new enthusiasm for stepping out and making a mark.

You need to assemble a crew of people who are smart, compassionate, and committed to your success. You want them to call you out if you shrink back from challenge, and cheer you on when you have a victory. They must do their own great work right by your side.

To select your crew, answer the question:

Whom do I need around me to strengthen my resolve, better my game, and get my back?

## Gather your reminders

One thing is certain: after you dig deep and find your root, clarify your vision of success, and assemble your crew, you will wake up one morning and forget everything.

All you will feel is loneliness and fear.

So you need symbols, sounds, and words to remind you of the passion you feel for making an impact with your work.

These can be photographs or soundtracks. Or letters from satisfied clients. Or rousing quotes from leaders you admire.

To find the right reminders for why you want to do great work, even when it is hard, answer the question:

Which images, songs, and words fire up my passion?

Great work does not flow only from the most talented, the most equipped, or the most worthy. It also flows from the people who believe they have the right to do it.

Why not you?

## PERSONAL BRANDING IS NOT OPTIONAL

More layoffs. Giving back bonuses. Fewer work days to save the company from firing people. Doing the job of the three people who were let go in your department. Not hiring the five people you were thinking about hiring. Trying to find a job in this climate....

Whether you are an employee in a big, medium, or small business, or an entrepreneur, or about to enter the workforce, never has it been more important to understand the power of having, maintaining, and developing a strong personal brand. Never before have there been more ways for you to connect and to build your personal brand through digital channels.

Never has a simple search on Google been able to tell us more about a person—who he is, what he does, and why he matters.

What does Google say about you?

If brands matter more than ever (and they do; just ask Apple, Starbucks, and Twitter), then the ability of individuals to build a personal brand has never been more important. Maybe the idea of "branding yourself" seems ridiculous. It's not. It's a subject that famed management guru and author Tom Peters first tackled fifteen years ago in a Fast Company article in which he wrote, "We are CEOs of our own companies: Me Inc. To be in business today, our most important job is to be head marketer for the brand called You."

Peters gave us the beginning of an insight: just as they do with big corporate brands, all of the people we connect with have some kind of similar emotions and thoughts when they think about us as people.

## MITCH JOEL

*Mitch Joel is President of Twist Image, an award-winning digital marketing and communications agency. His first book,* Six Pixels of Separation, *helps readers navigate business life in the relatively uncharted waters of social media and looks at new media and the new consumer. Follow Mitch on Twitter at @mitchjoel and on the Web at www.twistimage.com/blog. A version of this article first appeared in* The Vancouver Sun.

*Never has it been more important to understand the power of having, maintaining, and developing a strong personal brand.*

That mental tattoo that our personas and reputations create in their mind's eye is the essence of our personal brand.

But Peters wrote this in a world where individuals were limited by how they could spread their personal brands—the Internet was just taking its commercial shape in 1997. Now, in a world of blogs, Twitter, Facebook, and LinkedIn, our personal brands are resonating twenty-four hours a day, and the content we put online and link to says more about who we are, as individuals, than any one-page résumé ever could.

There's a small caution.

People working on their personal brand sometimes seem a little snake-oil salesy-like. They might state that they are working on their personal brand in a way that makes it look like they are trying too hard. They are the same kind of people who maneuver through the local Chamber of Commerce event, dumping business cards in any available and open hand.

No need to be that person.

The amazing thing about developing your personal brand online in social networks and by blogging is that you can hone in on connecting with those that have shared values and similar interests.

One of the best places to get started is with a search engine. Start looking for blogs in your industry, and start following some of the more notable people on Twitter. After you get a feel for the type of content people are publishing, you can dip your toes into the personal branding waters by leaving comments on those blogs or spaces. You can even go neck deep and start your own blog to demonstrate your own unique perspective.

Personal branding and the new media space create a unique and mutually beneficial relationship. Anyone can express who they are to the world. And if you're not sure what you have to say that is unique and different, just remember the immortal words of Oscar Wilde: "Be yourself, everyone else is already taken."

## THE KEYS TO KIVA

Kiva now has seventy staff members, two hundred fellows, and five hundred volunteers. We raised $1 million in our first year, and now we raise $1 million every five days. So we're growing fast. And people keep asking me—what's the secret to sustaining rapid growth?

It boils down to three key elements: growth, creativity, and feedback.

### Growth

First and foremost, people need someone who believes in their own growth. That's why we fly all of our fellows to San Francisco for a week of training, so they can become experts in microfinance. We also have a Kiva Fellows Alumni Program so that our alumni can connect with each other and get hooked up with jobs in development even after they've left the company.

We also invest in our core staff—we promote from within, provide executive coaching, and provide a brown-bag education series, and we do behavioral analysis with tools like the enneagram so that people can break free of their self-limiting blocks. For some people it's tough to open up and build trust, but it's worth it because that's how we can all grow together.

### Creativity

People need opportunities to be creative; it's absolutely vital. What I've learned is that if people feel like they need to paint by numbers, they'll work at one-third of their productivity level. So we've created a system in which once in every five iteration cycles, our engineers do an "innovation" iteration, in which they can release any kind of

## PREMAL SHAH

*Premal Shah is the President of Kiva.org, a nonprofit organization with a mission to connect people through lending to alleviate poverty. Premal helped found Kiva in 2005 after a sabbatical in India convinced him to leave his job at PayPal and pursue his passion for Internet microfinancing. Follow Kiva on Twitter at @kiva and on the Web at Kiva.org.*

*If people feel like they need to paint by numbers, they'll work at one-third of their productivity level.*

programming code they want. And what we've found is that they create three times as much code during the innovation iteration. People can experiment without asking for permission, and this creates a huge boost in morale.

We also allow the Kiva Fellows to write the bullets that appear on the home page of the website, so that everyone is co-creating the site, and people have a voice and gain visibility.

### Feedback

In a traditional corporate environment, people get an annual performance review and a bonus and salary increase that are very disconnected from the work they actually did. At Kiva, we have much shorter feedback loops. We have a monthly meeting where people stand up and talk for three minutes about their project, so they're getting immediate feedback. Our translators get a big kick out of translating a difficult passage for the community they serve; it gives them a great sense of accomplishment and pride. And when the translation goes up on the website, they're able to see results immediately when people from all over the planet start funding a loan. It's much more satisfying than getting a T-shirt or a phone call from me.

Finally, we work every day to keep people connected to our mission. One way we do this is by sending staffers out into the field to meet the people they're intending to serve. They are able to experience firsthand the impact that's being made, and that's how we keep increasing the quality of what we do.

## DREAM BACKWARD TO MOVE FORWARD

Most of us dream in the wrong direction.

When confronted with a job we don't love or a life that feels purposeless, we look forward to the future and ask big discovery questions:

What do I want to be when I grow up? What do I want to do with my life? What is my calling?

In that moment, the answer we get is often a little terrifying because every option in the world is on the table.

Should I get a new job?

Do I need to go back to school?

Could I volunteer more?

Start my own nonprofit?

Take up a new hobby?

Find a sport I enjoy?

What's my dream? What's my passion? What's my next move forward?

As we survey the black hole of endless possibility, we often get overwhelmed in that moment. We don't know where to start when we ask discovery questions, so we stop. We freeze. We get paralyzed and give up dreaming before we've even really begun.

But what if dreaming were an act not of discovery but of recovery? Of rescuing something from your past that was lost? Something

## JON ACUFF

*Jon Acuff is an author, speaker, launcher, and Dave Ramsey team member. Jon has written three books, including* Quitter: Closing the Gap Between Your Day Job and Your Dream *Job and* Stuff Christians Like. *Follow Jon on Twitter at @jonacuff and on the Web at JonAcuff.com.*

> *Finding your calling and your dream is not a first date; it is more often than not a reunion.*

you put down because life got too busy and dreams are usually the first thing to get bumped off the to-do list when the day gets full. Something that someone who mattered to you told you didn't matter. A teacher, a parent, or a peer said, "You're not good enough to do that. You could never turn that into a full-time job. You would never make enough money to live on." So you stopped.

A friend of mine used to love to dance when she was a little girl. It was all she dreamed about. In the eighth grade, her mom pulled her aside and said, "You know you're not going to be a Rockette, right? You know that's not in the cards for you, right?"

Do you think she danced much after that? Do you think it was easy for her to lean into that dream with everything she had? Of course not. She left her dream behind in the eighth grade.

Most of us have done the same thing in our own lives. We've felt something big and true but for a million reasons stopped doing it and left it in our past. That's why finding your calling and your dream is not a first date; it is more often than not a reunion. And if that's the case, if dreaming is an act of recovery and not an act of discovery, that changes everything.

Instead of asking forward-facing questions like "What do I want to do with my life?" we dream backwards and ask, "What have I done in my life that I've loved?" And the answer we get is not a bottomless, faceless list of options that could apply to anyone. It's a personal, small handful of life experiences that were uniquely tailored to our hearts and our souls and that made us feel alive.

And finding those life experiences—dreaming backwards—gives you everything you really need to move forward.

## FIND YOUR ELEMENT

How many people do you think have ever lived on earth? By "people" I mean homo sapiens, our own species, which emerged in our modern form about fifty thousand years ago. It's impossible to know for certain, of course, because no one has been counting until recently. But take a guess. It seems that the best estimates are between 60 and 110 billion people—let's say 80 billion as an average. Of those, almost 7 billion, including you and me, are living on the earth now. Collectively, we are the largest generation of human beings ever to live on the earth at the same time, and we make up somewhere between 8 and 10 percent of the total number of people who have ever lived.

Now think about how many of those 80 billion or so people had to meet each other and hang out, and in what different circumstances, during the course of those fifty thousand years, before your own parents ran into each other and eventually conceived you. The fact is, as the Dalai Lama puts it, being born at all is a miracle.

So congratulations: you made it.

And now that you are here, to quote the Dalai Lama again, what are you going to do with this brief life?

In my experience, many people settle for too little. They don't especially enjoy the work they do or the lives they lead. They get through the week and wait for the weekend. This isn't true of everyone, of course. There are many people who love what they do and couldn't imagine doing anything else. They live lives that resonate deeply with their true sense of who they really are. They are in their element, and

## SIR KEN ROBINSON

*Sir Ken Robinson, Ph.D., is an internationally recognized leader in the development of creativity, innovation, and human resources. To follow his best-selling book* The Element, *he is working on its sequel,* Finding Your Element. *Follow Sir Ken on Twitter at @sirkenrobinson and on the Web at sirkenrobinson.com, and see him speak at TED.com.*

*Finding your element is fundamental to living a life that has purpose and meaning.*

in my first book I argue that being in your element involves at least three processes.

The first is that when you're in your element, you're doing something for which you have a natural aptitude; the second is that you love it, too. This is essential. I know many people who are good at things they don't care for. Being in your element is more than being good at something. It is being at the place where talent meets passion. There is a third factor. Being in your element is also about connecting with others who share your passion: it's about finding your tribe.

Finding your element is fundamental to living a life that has purpose and meaning. Some people make a living from being in their element; others can't or don't want to. They are amateurs in the true sense of doing something purely for the love of it. Whichever is true for you, there are some issues to consider. If you have not found your element, why is that? Do you have any sense of what it might be and are you willing to explore the possibilities? If you do know what your element is and you're not in it, what's standing in your way?

I don't think there is a reliable twelve-step plan to being in your element that will guarantee the outcome. Human life isn't like that. But it is possible to offer some navigational tools for those who are committed to the quest. The first journey is inward. It begins with spending time with yourself: reflecting on the times in your life when you've felt most engaged, absorbed, or lost in the moment. You might make a list, or create a collage of images, or meditate, or try automatic writing, or do all of these to reconnect with your own interests, sensibilities, and sense of what fires your energy. The second journey is outward: to try new experiences that stretch your sense of capability, that may take you to new places, to new people, or at least to new ways of thinking and feeling.

One of the reasons that our species has come to dominate life on earth is that we have powerful imaginations and enormous capacities for creativity. As the largest generation in history so far, how well we use these capacities now will determine how many more people live on earth after us and in what circumstances. You may be one of 80 billion, but each of our lives, brief as it is, is unique and, to a large extent, of our own making. More than any other species, we create our lives, and we can re-create them. This is what Carl Jung had in mind when he said, "I am not what has happened to me. I am what I choose to become." As human beings we have many choices, and one of the most fundamental is whether or not to live in our element.

## I'M SCARRED

I got my first scars before I was a week old.

I was born with a cleft lip and palate, something I inherited from my Dad.

In my first couple of years, I had various operations that sewed up the top of the inside of my mouth (it's not smooth like yours, but has a crevasse) and sewed up the split in my top lip.

One of my two brothers has a cleft lip, and so does his son, so it's become something of a family tradition. In fact, when my youngest brother was old enough to realize that he'd been born without a cleft lip and palate, he burst into tears—he didn't want to be the odd guy out.

Being a large, enthusiastic, and clumsy guy, I didn't just stop there. I've spent the rest of my lifetime collecting a whole bunch of other scars.

Knees (endless soccer scrapes, including a run-in with one semi-buried brick in London), my hands (falling off bikes, my second date with my wife), my legs (a wire fence), my face (more bike crashes)... the list goes on.

And as I notice my scars now, there are two things I see.

The first thing I notice is that each scar has a story to it. It's the tattoo of an adventure. That white line between my ring finger and little finger? My second-date scar, a story involving mud, blood, stingy taxi drivers, abandonment, poetry, the loss of a treasure, a journey, and a happy ending.

## MICHAEL BUNGAY STANIER

*Michael Bungay Stanier is the founder of Box of Crayons, a company that helps people and organizations do less Good Work and more Great Work. His most recent book, if you don't count putting this book together, is* Do More Great Work: Stop the Busywork and Start the Work That Matters. *Follow Michael on Twitter at @boxofcrayons and on the Web at BoxOfCrayons.biz.*

*In the end, you get to regard your scars as a source of strength and wisdom, or as ties that bind.*

The other thing I notice is that my scars are the places that, although healed, remain a little tender and a little twisted. When you've been wounded, you don't go back to "the same as before." Things are a little different.

## Other scars

In some ways, the physical scars are the easy ones to notice—the rips and tears from bumping into things in life.

We're all carrying more subtle scars as well, emotional bruises from our past.

Times we've shamed or been shamed.

Times we've shunned or been shunned.

Times when we've failed or caused others to fail.

Times when we've let ourselves or others down.

These are older, deeper wounds, subtle and hidden. They can shape our behavior in significant ways.

We back away, not willing to try that again.

We lash out, preferring attack to being attacked.

We lose courage, we play it safe, we hide.

Your scars can hold you back and limit you. But there's another way to see them.

**A scar is a story waiting to be told**

In fact, two stories.

One story of love. And its flip side, one of fear.

One of nourishment. One of diminishment.

Which story you choose to tell matters a great deal.

Let me show you what I mean. Here are two stories I tell myself about my cleft lip and palate. They're both equally true.

### The story of fear

My cleft lip and palate means I have a speech impediment, an oddly shaped top lip, and a somewhat flattened nose.

People find me disconcerting to look at—some people see me as ugly.

People don't want to talk to me because they're uncomfortable about my cleft lip. Kids especially.

I should operate "behind the scenes" because my speech impediment means I shouldn't be "out front."

If I don't talk too much, people won't notice I have a disability. Stay quiet.

This is my disability.

**The story of love**

My cleft lip and palate means I have a speech impediment, an oddly shaped top lip, and a somewhat flattened nose.

I stand out from the crowd. I'm not bland.

People don't notice my speech impediment. They just accept me for who I am, especially when I do what I'm best at.

When I give speeches, my unique style of speaking helps me stand out from the crowd.

People find it easier to connect to me because I have an obvious vulnerability. It balances me out, and for some people, I can be a role model for overcoming "disabilities."

This is one source of my power.

Same scars. Same person. Very different stories.

I read somewhere that scar tissue is the strongest tissue in your body. It turns out that this is not scientifically true.

But it feels like it's true at a metaphysical level, doesn't it? I believe that where we've been wounded, and the scars we've collected along the way, could be a source of our greatness.

This idea also makes it clear that there is a choice to be made. Whatever the facts of the situation, you get to write the story about what it means. In the end, you get to regard your scars as a source of strength and wisdom, or as ties that bind.

I could ask you: What choice are you making?

But a more powerful question might be this:

There's a wound or a scar you have—physical or emotional—that you're currently using as a way of limiting who you are in this world and what you might be doing.

What is it? And what will it take for you to change perspectives?

# CREATE FREEDOM

*"Life is a series of collisions with the future; it is not the sum of what we have been, but what we yearn to be."*

José Ortega y Gasset,
Spanish writer and dissident

You know the scene from *Star Wars*—the first movie, the good one—where Luke and Han and the gang are trapped in the trash compactor? They survived being shot at by the Storm Troopers and then survived a brief flurry with a lurking creature, but now the walls suddenly start to move. Our trapped heroes do all they can to prevent themselves from being crushed, but it appears to be inevitable.

The contributors here are all asking you to embrace your inner R2-D2, the little robot who steps in and saves the day. Here's how you create and maintain both the physical and psychic space to allow vision, focus, and creativity to flourish, even as you feel like the walls are closing in.

## IN THIS SECTION

## IN A PERFECT WORLD...

Finish this sentence:

In a perfect world, _____.

It can be personal or business. For example:

"In a perfect world, I wake up in my house on the beach and just create new ideas all day long. The world finds those ideas useful and pays me to keep creating them."

Or, "In a perfect world, the fax machine is gone. When someone needs my legal signature, they email it to me. I enter my secret password, and my computer stamps it with my unique verified signature. Then I email it back."

You have hundreds of these. Write them down. The world is not supposed to be perfect as-is. If it were, we'd all be in heaven, playing harps in the clouds, with no reason to do anything.

By defining "a perfect world," you get a worthy To-Do list. In both personal and business matters, it's what we should all be aiming for.

On the personal side, this exercise makes you realize what kind of life you'd really like to be living, which is a great reminder for those thousand tiny daily decisions that can keep you pointed that way.

On the business side, it's the root of all great business ventures. The point of making a business is not to make money—it's to make your little corner of the world perfect.

## DEREK SIVERS

*Derek Sivers founded CD Baby and for doing so was labeled "a musicians' savior." Among his current projects is Muck Work, supporting creatives by doing their uncreative dirty work. Follow Derek on Twitter at @sivers and on the Web at Sivers.org, and see him speak at TED.com.*

If you let this mission guide all your decisions, you'll find a much more exciting focus than framing everything in the terms of today's very not-perfect world.

*Get a worthy To-Do list. It's what we should all be aiming for.*

## THE CHOICES THAT MATTER

Americans, and citizens of the developed West more generally, tend to take it for granted that more freedom is always better than less, and that more choice always means more freedom. Thus, we seek to "keep options open" in our own lives, and to offer options to our customers and clients. The logic seems incontrovertible: people who don't want all the options can ignore them, and people who do want them will be happy consumers. The more options, the better. Bring it on.

Logically true—perhaps. Psychologically true—not so much! Having too many options leaves many of us paralyzed with indecision. And when we do manage to decide, we are often dissatisfied with even good choices because we're convinced that a different option would have been better.

What does this tell us? As consumers of goods and services, we should seek to limit our options, not expand them. And as providers of goods and services, we should seek to curate, filter, and manage options so that our customers are liberated by the options we do offer and not tyrannized by them.

Have consumers and marketers of goods and services learned this paradoxical fact about choice? There is little reason to think so. Every day, the options expand—in cars, in cell phones, in TV stations, even in the kinds of pillows we can get in a hotel or the kinds of bottled water we can get in a restaurant. We continue to operate on the assumption that because some choice is good, more choice must be better.

Except in one area of life—managing our employees. Here, we seek to substitute rules for discretion, scripts for imagination. We don't trust

## BARRY SCHWARTZ

*Barry Schwartz is a professor of psychology at Swarthmore College in Pennsylvania, and is author and co-author of a number of books, including* The Paradox of Choice: Why More Is Less *and* Practical Wisdom: The Right Way To Do the Right Thing. *You can see Barry talk at TED.com.*

*We seek to substitute rules for discretion, scripts for imagination.*

our employees to use their judgment. In the world of human interaction, in which each situation is in some way unique, we take a one-size-fits-all approach to management. What scripted, micromanaged interactions do is that they protect against disaster but guarantee mediocrity. We fear that our corps of teachers has bad judgment and won't be able to figure out what each student needs. So we give them scripted lesson plans to follow. The result is that they miss the mark with every student. In addition, they are deprived of the opportunity to develop good judgment.

All human interactions demand judgment and wisdom, and the development of judgment and wisdom demands the freedom to choose, to make mistakes, and to learn from those mistakes. Employees who have the discretion to make choices will be better employees. And beyond that, they will also find more meaning and satisfaction in the work they do. They will be happier, more fulfilled people.

Thus, if we want more satisfied customers, we should limit the choices we offer to them. And if we want more effective and happier employees, we should increase the choices we offer to them. Less choice and discretion for our customers, and more choice and discretion for our employees. At the moment, we've got things exactly backwards.

## DON'T PAY ATTENTION

We live in a time that worships attention. When we need to work, we force ourselves to focus, to stare straight ahead at the computer screen. There's a Starbucks on seemingly every corner—caffeine makes it easier to concentrate—and when coffee isn't enough, we chug Red Bull. In fact, the ability to pay attention is considered such an essential life skill that the lack of it has become a widespread medical problem: nearly 10 percent of American children are diagnosed with attention-deficit hyperactivity disorder (ADHD).

In recent years, however, scientists have begun to outline the surprising benefits of not paying attention. Sometimes, too much focus can backfire; all that caffeine gets in the way. For instance, researchers have found a surprising link between daydreaming and creativity—people who daydream more are also better at generating new ideas. Other studies have found that employees are more productive when they're allowed to engage in "Internet leisure browsing," and that people unable to concentrate due to severe brain damage actually score above average on various problem-solving tasks.

Consider a 2011 study led by researchers at the University of Memphis and the University of Michigan. The scientists measured the success of sixty undergraduates in various fields, from the visual arts to science. They asked the students if they'd ever won a prize at a juried art show or been honored at a science fair. In every single domain, students who had been diagnosed with attention-deficit disorder achieved more; their inability to focus turned out to be a creative advantage.

And this lesson doesn't apply only to people with a full-fledged disorder. A few years ago, scientists at the University of Toronto and

## JONAH LEHRER

*Jonah Lehrer is the author of* How We Decide *and* Proust Was a Neuroscientist. *He's a Contributing Editor for Wired Magazine, Scientific American Mind, and National Public Radio's Radio Lab. Follow Jonah on Twitter at @JonahLehrer and on the Web at JonahLehrer.com.*

*When we're faced with a difficult problem, the most obvious solution—that first idea we're focused on—is probably wrong.*

Harvard University gave a short mental test to eighty-six Harvard undergraduates. The test was designed to measure their level of "latent inhibition," which is the ability to ignore stimuli that seem irrelevant, such as the air-conditioner humming in the background or the conversation taking place in a nearby cubicle. This skill is typically seen as an essential component of productivity since it keeps people from getting distracted by extraneous information.

Here's where the data get interesting: Those undergrads with low levels of latent inhibition—who had a tougher time ignoring unrelated stuff—were also seven times more likely to be rated as "eminent creative achievers" based on their previous accomplishments. (The association was particularly strong among distractible students with high IQs.) According to the scientists, the inability to focus helps ensure a richer mixture of thoughts in consciousness. Because these people struggled to filter out the world, they ended up letting everything in. They couldn't help but be open-minded.

Such lapses in attention turn out to be a crucial creative skill. When we're faced with a difficult problem, the most obvious solution—that first idea we're focused on—is probably wrong. At such moments, it often helps to consider far-fetched possibilities, to approach the task from an unconventional perspective. And this is why distraction is helpful: people unable to focus are more likely to consider information that might seem irrelevant but will later inspire the breakthrough. When we don't know where to look, we need to look everywhere.

This doesn't mean, of course, that paying attention isn't an important mental skill, or that attention-deficit disorders aren't a serious problem. There's clearly nothing advantageous about struggling in the classroom or not being able to follow instructions. (It's also worth pointing out that these studies all involve college students, and don't tell us anything about those kids with ADHD who fail to graduate from high school. Distraction might be a cognitive luxury that not everyone can afford.) Nevertheless, this new research demonstrates that for a certain segment of the population, distractibility can actually be a net positive. Although we think that more attention can solve everything—that the best strategy is always a strict focus fueled by triple espressos—that's not the case. Sometimes, the most productive thing we can do is surf the Web and eavesdrop on that conversation next door.

# WHAT CREATIVE TYPES ALREADY KNOW ABOUT PRODUCTIVITY

Creative types get typecast as meandering goal setters for a reason. They tend to ... meander. We resist structure (even though we crave it). We relish spontaneity (even though we're intrigued by five-year goal-setting plans). We tend to be driven by inspiration. We get there in our own way, and when the "flow" works, we're so smokin' productive that PERT charts and To-Do lists cringe in the wake of our creative productivity. Creatives have a thing or two to teach The Linears and The Planners. Here's an approach to creative productivity that works for artists and Type A personalities at work and in life:

## 1. Approach everything as a creative opportunity

There is no separation between life and work. The same opportunities to express yourself or discover great ideas are at the dinner table, in the stock exchange, and on the subway.

To keep your antennae up...

## 2. Obsession is essential

Know your art and your science. Immerse yourself in the cultures you love and work in: read industry news, read the teachings of spiritual masters and successful entrepreneurs, and listen to what the people you serve are longing for, asking for, and leaning toward.

## DANIELLE LAPORTE

*Danielle LaPorte is a creative type. She writes, consults, and teaches about the topic of creatively making a difference in the world as an entrepreneur. She is the author of* The Fire Starter Sessions. *Follow Danielle on Twitter at @DanielleLaPorte and on the Web at WhiteHotTruth.com.*

*Approach everything as a creative opportunity*

To foster obsession:

**2.1. Read a LOT of magazines.**

And then read some more ... about things related and unrelated to your work: Scientific American and Vogue, Dwell and Rolling Stone. Magazines are intensified viewpoints that can expand your perspective in just a few pages.

**2.2. Create a style file or inspiration box of stuff that you love**

Images, articles, fabric swatches. I have an antique sake box filled with strange and lovely stuff. Sometimes I close my eyes and reach in to see what surfaces—a saved concert ticket, a Zen koan torn from a divinity school program, notes from an old business plan—and I always get a fresh perspective or some idea affirmation.

**2.3. Watch dox.**

I'm a documentary-phile (always looking for versions of the truth). Documentaries give me all sorts of weird, tragic, and breathtaking imagery, inspiration, and facts to work with.

**2.4. Engage with people that you don't hang out with. Ask them big questions.**

Ask the cab driver what crazy stuff he's seen as a cab driver. Ask your friend's teenager what she thinks about the future. Ask your bank teller what it's like to work with money all day.

To keep moving forward...

### 3. Give up quickly

If something feels like a drag and is not generating the right response, drop it like a hot potato. As Seth Godin says in his book The Dip, "Fail fast."

In order to give up quickly, you have to...

### 4. Courageously express your feelings

When something feels very wrong, totally uninspiring, say so—to yourself and your team. It doesn't necessarily mean that you give up; it may spin you off into a better solution.

So that you can...

### 5. Stick with it

If something feels fun, glimmering, and exciting, and even one person has expressed wanting it from you, explore every angle about how to make it work.

And be assured that...

### 6. Backwards is forwards

Know that there is no such thing as waste. A painted canvas that didn't turn out, a pilot group that fizzled, it's all useful. I trash stuff and start from scratch often. Sometimes, especially in Web development, you start knowing that you'll have to scrap half of what you build down the road—starting over is never really starting over. It's life.

Which allows you to…

## 7. Celebrate other people's creativity and prosperity

Honoring other people's creativity and success shakes loose our own brilliance. Whether it's a hot website, your project manager, or a well-known author, go out of your way to say, "You're great!" "Way to go!" "I love what you've created."

And then keep on creating for yourself—ever so productively.

## GENIUS IS IN THE MARGINS OF YOUR ATTENTION

A decade or two ago, the complexity scientist Stuart Kauffman coined the phrase "adjacent possible" as a way of describing the way both human and biological systems are capable of changing. You can think of it as being like a chessboard in the middle of a game: at every point there is a finite set of moves that are possible, and a much larger set of moves that you cannot make.

So imagine a primordial soup with a few swirling atoms of various elements. The adjacent possible of that system is defined by all the various molecules that can be formed by those atoms. It's a very useful concept, because it works just as easily for cultural systems as it does for biological systems. When humans started walking upright, it opened up the adjacent possible for more complex tool use because our hands were freed up. When we invented vacuum tubes and integrated circuits, it opened up the adjacent possible for computers.

In our own lives, the trick is to figure out ways to explore your own personal adjacent possible: all the different ways your work or creative life can be recombined into new forms. In effect, the "patterns" of innovation that I wrote about in my book *Where Good Ideas Come From* are all, in one way or another, techniques for exploring the adjacent possible more effectively.

Unlocking new doors in the adjacent possible often comes out of making a new connection between seemingly unrelated fields. And so one key technique for opening your own mind up to new possibilities is to diversify your interests, and work on multiple projects in parallel.

## STEVEN JOHNSON

*Steven Johnson is an entrepreneur, author and speaker. He has written seven books, the most recent of which is* Where Good Ideas Come From: The Natural History of Innovation. *Follow Steven on Twitter at @stevenbjohnson and on the web at StevenBerlinJohnson.com.*

*New ideas are more likely to come out of those serendipitous discoveries that happen at the margins of your attention, in your hobbies and background pursuits.*

Many of the people I write about in the book were what I call "slow multitaskers." They weren't multitasking in the sense of switching back between email and Twitter every five seconds, but they worked on multiple projects simultaneously over longer periods of time, usually with very different subject matter, switching back and forth between them on the scale of hours or days. (Darwin's career was constantly in this mode.) That's an enormously generative work routine, because it enables you to make surprising new connections in your own private intellectual environment. I've experienced that multiple times in my own career: the idea for my hyperlocal web company outside.in came about because I was writing about 19th-century neighborhoods in my book *The Ghost Map*, but reading a lot of local blogs in Brooklyn, and simultaneously following some of the technical developments that were happening with Google's then newly-released Maps API. Something in the overlap between those three interests gave me the idea for outside.in.

In fact, one of the defining characteristics of the innovators that I profile in the book is the simple fact that most of them have a lot of hobbies. (Think of someone like Ben Franklin, who was constantly cycling through a huge range of diverse interests.) Hobbies have the generative effect of creating new potential connections to expand your main focus at work: either through direct links or through more metaphoric ways of approaching problems from new angles. So yes, there are times at work when you want to shut out the external world and really concentrate on a single problem. But every time you do that you make it harder to discover new openings in the adjacent possible.

New ideas are more likely to come out of those serendipitous discoveries that happen at the margins of your attention, in your hobbies and background pursuits. Focus is overrated.

## PERMISSION TO BE FUNNY

At lululemon athletica, we take humor very seriously—sometimes at the risk of baffling our customers. And we're very, very cool with that. We believe that Making Your Mark on the World means eliciting a few gasps of disbelief... followed by riotous, belly-quaking laughter.

Our company-wide April Fool's Day jokes are the stuff of legends.

A few years back, we "re-launched" our public website in the style of a Web 1.0 eyesore. Imagine every user interface design no-no under the sun, crammed onto a single splash page. That was our "new" site. Flashing sidebars, a black background with clunky lettering, pixelated images, and a cursor that trailed chintzy stars across the screen. It was a horrific thing to behold. And we thought it was absolutely hysterical.

We left the "re-branded" site up—for all the world to see—only until noon that day. Still, within a short period of time, perplexed messages from devoted customers poured in. We thanked them for their feedback and laughed until our abs were aching. (It was better than a 90-minute hot yoga class.)

Finally, we switched back to the real site, with a tongue-in-cheek apology to our customers. We think most of 'em got the joke. And as for the folks who didn't... well, there are always a few hecklers in every crowd.

Being unapologetically funny won't alienate your customers—or team members. Quite the opposite. Humor is about vulnerability. Vulnerability is about humanity. And at lululemon, we design our

## STEPH CORKER IRWIN

*Steph Corker Irwin proudly leads the Attraction team—magnetizing talent to join lululemon athletica on their quest to elevate the world from mediocrity to greatness. She is a believer in goal setting and dream chasing, and passionate about endorphin highs and sweaty pursuits. Namaste. You can follow Steph on Twitter at @SCorkerIrwin.*

business to support and sustain our humans—not the other way around.

Want to know our Top 5 Tips for weaving hardcore humor into your business plan, marketing strategy, or company culture? Drum roll, please....

*Don't whimper through the corner of your mouth—sing out!*

### 1. Keep it tasteful
Don't be patently offensive. That should go without saying.

### 2. Go big or go home
A half-hearted stab at humor won't resonate. Don't whimper through the corner of your mouth—sing out!

### 3. Be resourceful
Chances are, you've got some pretty hilarious people tucked away in quiet cubes and corner offices. Give them permission to be funny. And watch the brilliance bubble up.

### 4. Go buck-wild
There are no rules. Really.

### 5. Keep the faith
If every comedian quit after their first joke bombed, it'd be a pretty humorless world. Keep playing. Everything is progress.

## WHAT'S YOUR IDEA SCHEDULE?

Take a quick look at your schedule for the next two weeks. If you are like most people, your calendar is packed to the gills with endless appointments, meetings, conference calls, and deadlines. When, in this insanely busy schedule, are you planning to come up with your best ideas?

In the always-on, 24/7 business world we live in, when are we supposed to generate creative breakthroughs? In between checking our Blackberries, responding to email, and updating our Facebook status? There are countless hours scheduled for operations, sales, reporting, finance, efficiency gains, and human resources—yet very few people actually schedule time to think, create, and invent.

One busy executive schedules "Think Weeks" a few times a year. He goes off into seclusion for a week, loaded with reading material and time to explore his creativity. His staff waits with bated breath to hear about his newest ideas for the business. In fact, some of this company's most important advances originated during these Think Weeks. His name? The one and only Bill Gates. His legendary time to think left an indelible mark on Microsoft and was the source of some of their biggest innovations.

Which leads to my challenge to you: The 5% Challenge.

Instead of spending forty hours each week being "heads down," try taking 5 percent of your time (two hours each week) to be "heads up." Schedule time to explore the possibilities instead of cranking through assignments. This will have an immediate and incredibly powerful impact on your company, and on you as an individual.

## JOSH LINKNER

*Josh Linkner is on a mission to make the world more creative. Josh is the author of* Disciplined Dreaming: A Proven System to Drive Breakthrough Creativity, *a* New York Times *best-seller. Josh is the founder, Chairman, and former CEO of the largest interactive promotion agency in the world, ePrize. Josh is also the founder and CEO of Detroit Venture Partners, helping to rebuild Detroit through entrepreneurial fire. Follow Josh on Twitter at @JoshLinkner and on the Web at JoshLinkner.com.*

*When, in this insanely busy schedule, are you planning to come up with your best ideas?*

The 5% Challenge is easy to do: Get away from your desk and go to a place of inspiration, such as an art museum, park, or historic landmark. Turn off your phone and turn on your imagination. Give a siesta to your analytical, logical Left Brain, and let your creative, abstract Right Brain come out to play. Schedule the time and treat it with the same importance as any other business meeting. Show up fully, and let your imagination soar.

Scheduling just 5 percent of your week to reflect, think, and create can yield dramatic results. Many of the people I've convinced to give it a try report that they have become more efficient and more innovative at the same time. They also report that this is the most fun they have all week, and it is a time of both inspiration and renewal. The 95 percent of your time that you spend being task-oriented is actually more productive, while the 5 percent is a new gift to both you and your company.

Give it a try for thirty days. Two hours a week of unplugged, creative exploration. I have a hunch that it will quickly become one of your most important and rewarding habits. Before long, you'll be asking your friends and your colleagues, "what's your idea schedule?"

## BETA-THINK

Voltaire was half right. "Le mieux est l'ennemi du bien," he said: The best is the enemy of the good. The best is also the enemy of the better. Striving for perfection complicates and delays getting things done. Worse, the myth of perfection can shut off the process of improvement and the possibility of collaboration.

That myth of perfection is a byproduct of the industrial revolution and the efficiencies of mass production, distribution, and marketing. A product that takes a long time to design and produce is sold to a large market with a claim of perfection. Its manufacturer can't have customers think otherwise. The distribution chain invests in large quantities of the product and can't afford for it to be flawed. Money for mass marketing is spent to convince customers that the product is the best it can be. Thus perfection becomes our standard or at least our presumption. But perfection is delusion. Nothing and no one is perfect.

The modern cure to Voltaire's paradox—and a gift of the digital age—is the beta: the unfinished and imperfect product or process that is opened up so customers can offer advice and improvements. Releasing a beta is a public act, an invitation to customers to help complete and improve the product. It is an act of transparency and an admission of humility. It is also an act of generosity and trust, handing over a measure of control to others.

Google Vice President Marissa Mayer tells the story of the launch of Google News. It was near the end of the week. No online product is ever released on a Friday (if it breaks, your Saturday is ruined). So the team had just enough time before the weekend to add one more feature. They were debating whether to add a function to sort the news

## JEFF JARVIS

*Jeff Jarvis directs the Tow-Knight Center for Entrepreneurial Journalism at CUNY. He is the author of* What Would Google Do? *and* Public Parts. *Follow Jeff on Twitter at @jeffjarvis and on the Web at BuzzMachine.com.*

*That myth of perfection is a byproduct of the industrial revolution and the efficiencies of mass production, distribution, and marketing.*

by date or by place. They never got past debating. Come Monday, Google News came out as a beta (and stayed a beta for three years). That afternoon, Mayer says, the team received 305 emails from users, 300 of which begged for the ability to sort by date.

By admitting they weren't finished, the company heard from customers what to do next. "We make mistakes every time, every day," Mayer confesses. "But if you launch things and iterate really quickly, people forget about those mistakes and have a lot of respect for how quickly you build the product up and make it better." Beta is Google's way of never having to say they're sorry.

Beta-think can benefit more than technology products. I see betas coming from companies in fashion, restaurants, even chocolate and automotive. I wish we'd see more beta-think—more innovation, experimentation, and risk—from government, but bureaucrats and politicians are loath to admit imperfection. I also wish that education would operate under beta-think, encouraging learning by failure rather than teaching to a test and a perfect score of right answers. Beta-think can change how we think as managers. It can even change marriage (so much for trying to find the perfect husband or fix all his imperfections).

Beta-think opens an enterprise to the surprising generosity of the public. Look at the value that users build into Wikipedia, TripAdvisor, Yelp, and other services they control. Beta-think improves an institution's relationship with its public. Making errors—and confessing and correcting them quickly—will enhance rather than diminish credibility.

Once the fear of imperfection is taken out of the equation, innovation can flourish. Look at how Zappos improved customer service by letting employees make their own decisions (and mistakes). What does beta-think do to competitiveness? How can you show your hand to your rivals? That depends on where you see your real value: in keeping secrets from customers or in building strong relationships of trust by listening to and collaborating with them. Beta-think also brings speed. Even perfectionist Apple released its iPhone aware that it was incomplete, promising missing pieces in future updates.

Here's the wonderful irony of beta-think: It says that we can make what we do ever better because we are never done, never satisfied, always seeking ways to improve by working in public.

This essay, too, is a beta. It's not perfect. I'm not done with it. So please come to www.buzzmachine.com/beta-think and help make it better.

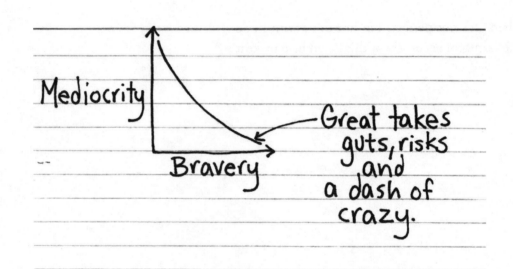

Mediocrity

Bravery

Great takes guts, risks and a dash of crazy.

# COURAGE

*Every 45 seconds, a child dies of malaria—but you can help change that.*

*Malaria is preventable and treatable.*

# LOVE & BE KIND

*"Kindness is more important than wisdom, and the recognition of this is the beginning of wisdom."*

Theodore Isaac Rubin,
Writer

When you recognize someone, before you're even conscious of it, something peculiar happens. Your eyebrows twitch a little, lifting slightly at the outside ends. It's a hard-wired neurological response to that "I know you..." moment, and it triggers endorphins and feel-good chemicals.

The philosopher Martin Buber frames it like this: our existence breaks down into just two types of relationships. The first is an I/It relationship, in which you stop seeing people for who they are and you objectify them, losing sight of their humanity. The second type of relationship is an I/Thou relationship, in which you see people for who they truly are, without labels and without boundaries.

In this section, the ongoing theme is to remember that those around you—your peers, team members, bosses, clients, customers, friends, and family—are all human beings.

## IN THIS SECTION

## THE STRENGTH OF VULNERABILITY

In our culture, vulnerability has become synonymous with weakness. We associate vulnerability with emotions like fear, uncertainty, and scarcity—emotions that we don't want to discuss, even when they profoundly affect the way we live, work, and even lead.

To reduce our feelings of vulnerability, we wake up every morning, put on our game face, and rarely take it off—especially in our work lives. We use invulnerability as a shield to protect us from discomfort, anxiety, and self-doubt.

The invulnerability shield takes on many shapes and forms. Some of us protect ourselves with perfecting, pretending, and pleasing. We convince ourselves that making everything "just right" and keeping everyone around us happy will minimize our risk of feeling blamed, judged, or criticized. Even though perfecting is exhausting and ultimately leads to resentment and blame, we keep thinking, "Maybe I just need to be a little more perfect."

Invulnerability can also take the form of low-grade disconnection. We protect ourselves by never quite being "all in." We never get too excited or too attached or too hopeful. We're always waiting for the other shoe to drop. The motto becomes, "It's easier to live disappointed than it is to feel disappointed."

Cruelty is both a type of invulnerability shield and the outcome of a culture that is collectively losing its tolerance for vulnerability. In a world facing political, environmental, economic, and social uncertainty, we rage and humiliate to discharge our own fear and anxiety. Rather than doing the difficult work of embracing our own vulnerabilities and imperfections, we expose, attack, and ridicule what is

## BRENÉ BROWN

*Brené Brown is a research professor at the University of Houston Graduate College of Social Work. She has spent the past ten years studying vulnerability, courage, authenticity, and shame, and she writes about them in her book,* The Gifts of Imperfection: Let Go of Who You Think You're Supposed To Be and Embrace Who You Are. *Follow Brené on Twitter at @BreneBrown and on the Web at BreneBrown.com, and see her speak as part of the TEDx series.*

*Vulnerability is equal parts courage, mindfulness, and understanding—it's being "all in."*

vulnerable and imperfect about others. We see this everywhere, from political talk shows and school meetings to the sidelines of kids' soccer games. Finger-pointing, screaming, and in-your-face personal attacks have replaced respectful debate and discourse.

The shield of invulnerability can protect us; however, never putting it down means never letting ourselves be seen. Invulnerability means always being guarded and staying closed to the most important human experiences.

Why is vulnerability worth the risk? Vulnerability is indeed at the core of difficult emotions, but it is also the birthplace of love and belonging, joy, creativity and innovation, authenticity, adaptability to change, and accountability—the experiences that bring purpose and meaning to our lives.

Cultivating relationships, finding meaning in our work, and reclaiming our creativity mean finding the courage to let our selves be seen. If we choose invulnerability, we have to settle for a type of counterfeit connection that often comes from being what we think we're supposed to be, rather than being who we are.

Vulnerability is not weakness; it is our strongest connection to humanity and to each other. Choosing vulnerability means leaning into the full spectrum of emotions—the dark as well as the light—and examining how our feelings affect the way we think and behave. Vulnerability is equal parts courage, mindfulness, and understanding—it's being "all in."

## THE BEST MARKETING STRATEGY EVER

Want to know the best marketing strategy ever?

It's simple, and you don't need an MBA or focus groups or endless market research to figure it out. Ready?

Care.

I told you it was simple. You need to care about your customers. The problem is that most people literally don't care. I mean, they want to sell more or they care for the sake of converting on the back end. But when consumers genuinely feel cared for, they'll be the advocates that build your business.

You don't need to worry about outspending your competition. You need to out-care your competition, and if you don't, someone else will come along and out-care you.

Why does the customer matter so much? The truth is, it's always been about the customer, and anybody who doesn't think so has no idea what they're talking about. And today, the customer's voice is louder than ever, and word-of-mouth travels farther than ever.

Your customers will talk about you on Facebook, Twitter, and Tumblr, whether you like it or not. If I get one bad haircut, I can tell thousands of people on Twitter and write a negative review on Yelp. Same goes for a great slice of pizza—it used to be that I would tell a couple of friends about good pizza. Now I can tell thousands of people in an instant.

Here's the catch: caring about the customer is a mindset, not a tactic. And it's got to come from the top. Whether you're in a billion-dollar

## GARY VAYNERCHUK

*Gary Vaynerchuk is the creator of the Wine Library and Wine Library TV, founder of VaynerMedia, and a force in social media. He is also the author of two books,* Crush It! *and* The Thank You Economy. *You can follow Gary on Twitter at @garyvee and on the Web at GaryVaynerchuk.com.*

*We're now in a marketplace where every whisper about your business gets heard.*

company or a small shop, the boss needs to step up and create a culture of caring within your four walls. Once you have the mindset of caring, and it becomes second nature to consider the customer in every decision, you can't lose.

There's a major cultural shift happening. Because people are more connected than ever on the Web, we're going back in time and living under small-town rules.

In a small town, businesses are friendly and caring and they go above and beyond because they know that your voice within that town is powerful. One person inside a town of 500 people or 5,000 people or even 25,000 people is more powerful than one voice in New York City.

This is a monumental shift—we're now in a marketplace where every whisper about your business gets heard. This means that corporations need to recognize that their bottom lines are going to be completely connected to their hearts, not their brains. Caring about the customer, caring about the story of your brand, and (of course) having a strong product are becoming more important than having the lowest price.

The challenge is that there are a lot of distractions that keep us from connecting with customers. But you have to do it, instead of just talking about it. When you commit to making true engagements, that's when the rubber hits the road.

For me, it means that when I'm at a wine event in Boston tonight, I'll spend several hours responding to emails from fans during my downtime at my booth. I could watch a DVD or surf the 'Net. But instead I'll connect with people.

No excuses, no distractions. Crush it!

## WORK IS A FOUR-LETTER WORD

I hear the snickers already. Elevate your minds. I've got another word that we often don't attach to work. It is a word of redemption, of contribution, of achievement, of community, and ultimately, of legacy.

Here it is: LOVE.

Kahlil Gibran said, "Work is love made visible." My version of Gibran: "A job is what you do for a paycheck. Work is what you do for a life."

Work is that energizing, all-encompassing activity that allows you to bring skills to bear in ways that are satisfying beyond a pay period. It is that activity that saves you from being a faceless number in a mechanistic wheel. It is that activity which makes a contribution to a larger world order. It is that activity from which you feel a measure of accomplishment and achievement. It excites you. It gives you joy. It binds you to a community of people who are stakeholders in what you do. Ultimately, it has a ripple effect and the potency of a legacy for those who follow.

"Yeah right," you mutter. "Mike Rowe is making a fortune on his reality show 'The World's Dirtiest Jobs.' You can't tell me that love is involved in THOSE jobs!"

Great point! It seems that not every employment opportunity has such grand potential. Just take the money, and leave the job as soon as you can for greener pastures. Screw those miserable bosses. Thumb your nose at the customer.

Or maybe you feel like a dead (wo)man walking, hating what you do but too scared to jump. A wobbly economy whiplashes everyone. Wall Street meltdowns, corporate greed, and icon-like presidents

## EILEEN MCDARGH

*Eileen McDargh works with people all over the world to teach them to be resilient and engaged both at work and at home. She is an internationally acclaimed speaker and the author of a number of books, including her latest,* Gifts from the Mountain: Simple Truths for Life's Complexities. *Follow Eileen on Twitter at @macdarling and on the Web at EileenMcDargh.com.*

*Work is that energizing, all-encompassing activity that allows you to bring skills to bear in ways that are satisfying beyond a pay period.*

who crash as fallen idols make daily headlines. Just hunker down and wait it out.

And tomorrow you die.

That's it. Plain and simple. While you are looking for the dream vocation, the better work environment, the nicer boss, reality can step in, and your one moment on Planet Earth is gone forever. Your life is over. Kaput. Dead. You're outta here.

Wouldn't it make more sense to transform wherever you find yourself—even while continuing to search—so that if and when you leave, there's a faint footprint of achievement, community, contribution, and yes, even the memory of a beneficial interaction? Such a transformation allows you to love yourself in the process. It keeps bridges from burning and strengthens a network of relationships that one day you might call upon.

The critical question becomes: how do you turn a "job" into a "work"—into something that gives you more than a paycheck? No, you might not be able to alter the corporate strategic plan, paint the garbage truck peppermint pink, or change a boss from a toad to a prince. But there are specific actions you can take within your sphere of influence.

### 1. Control the controllable

Stop wasting energy over situations, events, or people whom you cannot control. Ask yourself what is within your sphere of influence, and handle that and nothing else! I can't control an earthquake but I can be prepared.

## 2. Make it a game

Games involve skill, speed, accuracy, strategy, fun, AND scorekeeping. For decades, Charles Coonradt, author of The Game of Work and CEO of The Game of Work LLC, has consistently shown that the very components of recreational enjoyment can be replicated in the workplace.

## 3. Think contribution

If this were your last day on earth, what action could you take to make a contribution to someone or some thing? It might be small. Example: You called the hotel maid by name and wrote her a note (along with a tip) about how much you appreciated her effort. You paid the toll for the car behind you. You helped an administrative assistant collate a report so she could go home to her kids. At the end of the day, write in a blank journal (labeled "deposits") and describe the contribution you made. You're storing up a treasure that won't be affected by the stock market.

## 4. Practice intelligent optimism

This is the skill of reframing—of taking the difficult, the dirty, or the depressing and asking if there might be another way to see this. How could you reframe the event or the person? Example: "It's not a bad hair day. It's a GREAT hat day." Or think of this: "She's not a horrid boss. She's teaching me everything I want to learn NOT to do when I am a manager."

Got the idea? Don't wait. Time is too precious to squander. You CAN fall in love again.

## JUST MAKE IT UP

A conversation with a stranger typically doesn't begin with a thirty-minute prep session.

You don't have that option. It's live, unscripted, and raw. It's now or never.

You don't bump into a beautiful girl on the streets of New York while waiting in line for your ice cream and tell her, "Hold on. I don't have anything to say to you yet; let me just go and prepare something witty, serious, and with a dash of sincerity and I'll be right back."

What would that do to seal the deal and get her number? It would ruin it. You squashed the magic, the excitement, the joy from a brief and fragile encounter. She thinks you're weird, awkward, and worse: fake.

But we do the same thing with selling. We spoil the magic by thinking that selling is a forced conversation, one that is heavily scripted.

I liken selling to having an authentic, purposeful conversation in which you are yourself, not some "other" version that you save only for sales pitches.

But a great many people overcompensate with unnecessary preparation (stalling) and worry (fear) so that the conversation feels rigid, forced, and bottle-necked. They squander gems of opportunity.

They run back to their mental files of appropriate responses and nervously spew off, "Thank you. Any further inquiries regarding the cost, vendor location, and/or materials of this scarf can be obtained by emailing me at Iblewthesale@gmail.com."

## LAURYN BALLESTEROS

*Lauryn Ballesteros is a gutsy impresario, marketer, artist, and all-around sales ninja. She is currently the VP of Strategic Partnerships at The Domino Project, where she works with cutting-edge companies to help them use books as effective marketing tools. Follow Lauryn on Twitter at @heyLaurynbee and on the Web at LaurynBallesteros.com.*

*There is no secret. I'm myself, I believe in what I do, and I make up the rest as I go along*

And just like that, they lost an opportunity. They had a real moment to connect, one where the pretty girl reached out to make eye contact with them to see that they're real people, and they looked the other way.

The truth of the matter is that the sale (especially in large sales) happens when people trust you and there is a connection. And a great conversation is a phenomenal way to initiate that trust, but it's difficult to achieve if you are nothing but the reader of a script filled with overly professional jargon. Connection is at the heart of anything we do, and selling is no exception.

Great conversations are natural and unplanned. They're impromptu. In essence, they're made up, although we don't like to call them that because that would seem unprofessional or absurd. In fact, that is what a true conversation is! It's acting in the moment with purpose and intent while allowing yourself to shine through. And that, you can't script.

I can prepare only so much for my upcoming talk with Nike, because at the end of the day, human beings make the decisions (not this vague concept of "Nike" as a brand), and until I speak to those people, I will only be able to guess at what they value and who they are. And without that information, I am in a difficult position to understand their needs and thereby sell anything.

So when people ask me what my secret is in sales, my not-so-impressive response is, "There is no secret. I'm myself, I believe in what I do, and I make up the rest as I go along."

## HERE'S TO THE HATERS

Most companies want to be loved.

They want passionate customers, enthusiastic vendors, and devoted partners. They want engaged and loyal employees.

Yet in reality, pathetically few companies are loved. Most companies are tolerated at best, and ignored at worst.

Why? Most companies are too forgettable to be loved. They're too boring to spark a reaction— any reaction.

If you want your company to have passionately devoted customers, partners, and employees, you must first inspire strong responses. Only then can you convince people to love your company and become raving fans of your brand.

### The Lovers

Crazy-excited fans may be a small slice of your overall base, but they're the single most powerful force in your marketing mix. As customers, the Lovers not only purchase your product, but also invest in your stock, tolerate your mistakes, and refer you to their peers. As employees, they shape the culture, do extraordinary work, and change the game.

Lovers will reward you with new business, higher sales, and better talent.

But as you attract these raving fans, you'll also get the opposite: the critics and the naysayers. You'll get the Haters.

## SALLY HOGSHEAD

*Sally Hogshead helps companies develop messages that persuade and captivate. Her most recent book is* Fascinate: Your 7 Triggers to Persuasion and Captivation. *Follow Sally on Twitter at @sallyhogshead and on the Web at SallyHogshead.com.*

## The Haters

Haters add negative energy to your brand. The customers might post unpleasantries online or write nasty letters. The employees will push back, resist, and stop the easy flow of progress.

They're passionate, yeah, but in the opposite way than you'd like.

But let me say something rather shocking. Not only is it okay to have a few people hate your brand; it's absolutely necessary.

If you're not eliciting a negative response from someone, then you're probably not very compelling to anyone.

Dealing with rabble-rousers and critics is the price of entry for being extraordinary. You can deal with them directly, or even coax them to change, but do not let them stop you.

Accept their presence. See them, in fact, as a measure of success, and move on with your mojo intact.

So on one side, we have the Lovers. On the other side, we have the Haters. Between them is a no-man's land filled with dead ends and disengagement. This is where you'll find those lukewarm lollygaggers who suck up your time, effort, and resources but give little loyalty or value in return. These are the Middlers.

## The Middlers

Remember that slacker college buddy who commandeered your dorm-room La-Z-Boy to enjoy your subscription to Cinemax, but would always leave when you ran out of cheese puffs? Sorta like a friend, but not really. In the same way, lukewarm customers make an occasional purchase, but don't really add value.

> *If you're not eliciting a negative response from someone, then you're probably not very compelling to anyone.*

In a brutally competitive environment, you can't afford to waste your time talking to people who don't care. Unlike Lovers, who are devoted to you, these consumers are gigolos, switching to the most attractive offering. So in addition to being unreliable, Middlers are also expensive.

Yet consumers aren't the only ones loitering in the middle and damaging your business. Employees in the middle don't care about doing much other than killing time at the office. Clients in the middle don't really care about loyalty if your competitor offers a better price. Stockholders in the middle don't care about sticking with you in a downturn.

In a competitive environment, the middle position is death. Not caring is not buying. Not caring is inaction. Not caring is goodbye. There are too many options on the shelves, too many ways to shut out your advertising message, too many competitors who are more than happy to take your best clients and distributors and salespeople away if "don't care" is the best you can do.

How can you get people out of the middle? Once people stop being in the middle, they stop roaming aimlessly and start actively choosing you and your brand. That's when good things like sales and retention and leadership happen.

If your company wants to influence purchase decisions, you must provoke strong and immediate emotional reactions. The goal isn't to avoid controversy, but to avoid creating legions of people who simply don't care.

Stop focusing on the Middlers.

Stop letting the Haters slow you down.

Start rewarding, and keeping, the Lovers.

## THREE WORDS FROM ANN LANDERS

People say marketing is an external task. It's getting current and potential customers to have an open mind about a purchase. However, marketing is internal as well. We are always marketing. It's not a task or an action item or a position. Internal marketing can be referred to as HR, but then we take a different approach. We try to see how we can "manage" people, which makes it sound like it's a chore.

In reality, those employees, and you, might be the strongest or the weakest marketers within the company, but your impact is the greatest.

No one ever said, "This product is terrible, but they have a great mission statement, so I'm going to buy from them again! They really 'strive for market synergy!'"

It's the small things that are the big things. And internally, that means communication.

Take these three words that Ann Landers recommended as a test and try them with your team for one day (I dare you):

> Good. True. Helpful.

If what you're about to say or email to someone doesn't meet two out of those three criteria, reword it or don't say it at all.

Instead of saying "Late again, eh?" you can say "Mike, you're a valuable member of this team, and when you're late it holds up everyone's progress. What can I do to help you?"

I'm not even asking for three out of three.

## SCOTT STRATTEN

*Scott Stratten is the President of UnMarketing. He's one of the key influencers on Twitter and has created viral videos that have been seen more than 60 million times. He's the author of* UnMarketing: Stop Marketing. Start Engaging. *Follow Scott on Twitter at @unmarketing and on the Web at UnMarketing.com, and see him speak at TED.com and as part of the TEDx series.*

*Good. True. Helpful.*

Following this rule is harder than you think. Sarcasm, one of the leading forms of workplace communication, doesn't qualify under this rule. Neither does back-stabbing, gossip, or pettiness.

Imagine that you got rid of those issues for a day; what would your team dynamics be like? Heck, you may want to try it for a week or ten.

## PURSUING EXCELLENCE

If you know me at all, you know I stand for Excellence. Over the years, I've learned that achieving excellence is kind of like losing weight. It's the small changes—like taking the stairs instead of the elevator—that add up to make a difference.

Here are five connected ways you can pursue excellence and ensure that you create impact and meaning in the work you do.

### 1. Know that your calendar never lies

The most precious asset you have is your time. Your calendar is a truthful representation of what you think is important.

You need to know how the hell you're spending your time before you can decide whether you're spending it well. You need to keep track in a rigorous way, like a train conductor, checking at the end of the day, week, and month to see how you're spending your time.

If you're a manager and you give a speech about how the team has to work on improving the quality of output in the next quarter, but then you spend only six hours on it, it's not a priority.

Find someone you trust to look at your calendar (it can be a colleague, your spouse, or even a drinking buddy) and give you an honest assessment of whether you're spending your time on the most important things. The calendar tells the truth!

### 2. Step away from the computer

And no doubt, your calendar will tell you that you spend lots of time in front of a screen. I'm just about to pass five thousand tweets, so I'm doing pretty well for an old guy. But it's so critical to get away from

## TOM PETERS

*If there's such a thing as an über-guru, Tom Peters is probably it. He's written numerous influential books, starting with* In Search of Excellence *in 1982 and writing, most recently,* The Little Big Things: 163 Ways to Pursue Excellence. *Follow Tom on Twitter at @tom_peters and on the Web at TomPeters.com.*

electronic connectivity from time to time. You don't need to go on a Zen Buddhist retreat, but you need space to think. You've got to take a scrub rug to your brain, so you can return refreshed and recharged.

### 3. Daydream

What will help refresh you is daydreaming. I was reminded about the importance of this by Dov Frohman, a top executive at Intel Israel and godfather of Israel's high-tech industry. You can guess that this is likely a tough job in a disciplined company. But in his book Leadership the Hard Way, he says that "everything exciting comes from a daydream." Daydreaming is an effective way of coping with complexity. Every child knows how to daydream, but we lose the capacity for it as adults. Take time out for daydreaming—it's where you can find the seeds of excellence.

### 4. Consider the hang-out factor

While you're thinking about your calendar, take time to consider whom you hang out with. Did you know that you act like the six people that you're closest to? If you look at your current gang, this can obviously be very good news or very bad news.

Seek out new people. And while you're hanging out with them, learn how to listen. We don't have any problem with the notion of being a professional athlete, but I think being a professional listener is just as important.

### 5. Remember K = R = P

And finally, remember this as you work with people both familiar and new:

*Take time to consider whom you hang out with. Did you know that you act like the six people that you're closest to?*

Kindness = Repeat Business = Profit.

The epigraph of my most recent book is a quote by American states-man Henry Clay: "Courtesies of a small and trivial character are the ones which strike deepest in the grateful and appreciating heart." You can be a tough son of a gun in business but be decent and kind and thoughtful.

Kindness is free. Thoughtfulness is free. And people will remember that kindness thirty years later.

# DISRUPT NORMAL

*"You are remembered for the rules you break."*

Douglas MacArthur,
Soldier

Normal is expected.

Normal is comfortable.

Normal is safe.

Normal is OK.

Normal is predictable.

Normal is the status quo.

Normal is playing it safe.

Normal is overrated.

# IN THIS SECTION

## DON'T BE THE BLAND LEADING THE BLAND

It doesn't seem fair that an idea's worth is judged by how well it's communicated, but it happens every day. So it comes down to this: If you can communicate an idea well, you have the power to persuade.

The enemy of persuasion is obscurity. If you have an important message to get out, it must stand out, not blend in. Most presentations today err by being boring and bland—but with a little work, your ideas can get the attention they deserve.

You can learn what attracts attention by examining the opposite: camouflage. The purpose of camouflage is to reduce the odds that someone will notice you—and to do this by blending into the environment. But when is blending in appropriate for a communicator?

Never.

The more you want your idea adopted, the more it must stand out. If the idea blends with the environment, both its clarity and its chances for adoption are diminished. An audience should never be asked to make decisions based on unclear options.

So don't blend in; instead, clash with your environment. Stand out. Be different. That's what will draw attention to your ideas. Nothing has intrinsic attention-grabbing power by itself. The power lies in how much something stands out from its context.

There are a few simple ways to make your idea stand out:

## NANCY DUARTE

*Nancy Duarte is improving the impact of presentations. She is the CEO of Duarte Design, a firm focused on developing presentations that change the world. She wrote* Slide:ology *and* Resonate. *Follow Nancy on Twitter at @NancyDuarte and on the Web at Duarte.com.*

### 1. Establish a clear gap

Create the gap between what is (the current realities) and what could be (the world with your idea adopted). Verbally paint a picture of the current status quo juxtaposed with the glorious future in which your idea has been adopted.

### 2. Take a strong and clear position on a topic

This opens up the opportunity to compare your idea with opposing positions. Create compelling counter-arguments to your idea. Repeatedly contrasting your ideas with alternative ideas will make your idea more alluring.

### 3. Have passion for your idea.

Many communicators lack passion, so your passion will help you stand out. Lift your message out of the drab, traditional way that messages are typically communicated in your organization. Create fascination with and passion about your idea.

Presentations today are boring because there is nothing interesting happening. They are bland, so interest is lost. Your job as a communicator is to create and resolve tension through contrast. Building highly contrasting elements into communication holds the audience's attention.

If you aren't inspired by what you do—or if you don't have a message to convey that you're passionate about—find your calling. Find what inspires you and communicate it passionately in a way that stands out.

*You can learn what attracts attention by examining the opposite: camouflage.*

## THINKING WAS RUINING MY LIFE

My story is very personal, and hopefully much more extreme than anything you have gone through or ever will go through.

About a year ago I hit an all-time low, at work and in life. I was working at an amazing company and was surrounded by amazing and genuinely good people.

But after a while, it didn't matter; my thoughts had completely taken over. I ended up taking a leave of absence that lasted for three and a half months. I've been back for a while now and am in absolute heaven. It's the same group, same company, but a completely different experience. What did change is how I think and behave in my life. I learned a lot during my leave; I hope some of what I learned can be helpful for you or someone you know.

Here are some examples of how my thinking changed in productive ways:

THOUGHT: Thinking about doing something is useful.

REALITY: Taking action, even if it's a baby step, is much more useful, and a feeling of achievement comes with it.

THOUGHT: I have to be perfect.

REALITY: Perfection is unachievable and nobody wants to be around a perfectionist. Also, if you remain a perfectionist, you won't ever achieve up to your full ability because the fear of messing up will prevent you from fully exploring the possibilities.

## RYAN VANDERBILT

*Since graduating from Syracuse University, Ryan Vanderbilt has worked for four innovative companies. Landor, G2, Anomaly and Google. He loves to observe behaviors, watch interactions, see how things work or don't work, and try come up with smarter solutions. He has a passion for creating things and is honored and excited to be a part of this book.*

*Perfection is unachievable and nobody wants to be around a perfectionist.*

THOUGHT: If someone else is good at something that I am not good at, I need to learn it and become better.

REALITY: Focus on the things you are passionate about. Don't get caught up in the "one up, one down" mindset. Also, being good at a lot of things but not great at anything is not a path to success or personal fulfillment.

THOUGHT: Someone else must have already thought of that, so I won't say it.

REALITY: Surprisingly, even if something seems obvious to you, it might not be to anyone else, and you don't want to live with that feeling of "what if..." that you will have if you don't speak up.

THOUGHT: They must know I'm frustrated.

REALITY: Most people are very caring and want the best for you, but they are not mind readers, so you need to speak up.

THOUGHT: I'm not the right person to answer this.

REALITY: That's never true; if you have an opinion, then you are the right person.

THOUGHT: Asking for help will make me vulnerable.

REALITY: It's actually more of a sign of confidence than anything else.

THOUGHT: Being an expert is important.

REALITY: Sometimes the naive person is the best person to solve a problem because he doesn't have any baggage getting in the way of his ideas.

THOUGHT: Failing is bad.

REALITY: Failing is a positive thing. It means you took action. It's the only way to learn.

THOUGHT: I need to wait to be asked.

REALITY: You might never be asked, so just start doing it.

THOUGHT: Having fun at work means I'm not being productive.

REALITY: This is painfully wrong. To be creative and to generate ideas, you have to be in a positive mindset. Playing and having fun are vital for that.

THOUGHT: Other peoples' anger, tension, outbursts, and bad moods have something to do with me.

REALITY: Those are their issues; I can be sympathetic without personalizing the other person's behavior or mood.

THOUGHT: I have to be prepared to start.

REALITY: You will never feel fully prepared, so start anywhere.

THOUGHT: I have to focus on improving my faults and weaknesses.

REALITY: Put more focus on taking your passions and strengths to the next level.

THOUGHT: I have to please others at my own expense.

REALITY: You can't actually please others if you aren't happy.

THOUGHT: I can ignore a problem and it will go away, or I'll deal with it later.

REALITY: The problem doesn't go away until it's dealt with, and the longer you wait, the bigger and more distracting it becomes.

THOUGHT: Trying to anticipate all possible scenarios is a good form of being prepared.

REALITY: It's mostly a waste of time and energy, and it causes anxiety.

THOUGHT: I have to say yes to everything I'm asked to do, to show that I'm a team player.

REALITY: If you say yes to everything, you devalue yourself. This is one of my favorite quotes; it's from Jim Rohn: "If you don't design your own life plan, chances are you'll fall into someone else's plan. And guess what they have planned for you? Not much."

## THE BIGGEST DISTANCE IN THE WORLD

My son and I have an ongoing tease between us: "Ian, what's the biggest distance in the world?" "I know, I know, Dad. It's the distance between 'I know' and 'I do.'"

That exchange was designed to help an adolescent, then teenager, then adult, realize that—although I will always be there for him—most often he knows what to do; he just needs to search inside himself for the courage or wisdom to do it.

And this is the biggest distance I see in the work world. I see the same thing in Kansas City that I have seen in San Francisco, Milan, Hong Kong, Toronto, Brussels, London, and Detroit. Few do what they know they should, what they know they could, what they know truly matters. Instead, most insist on getting caught up in the crap, the clutter, and the tyranny of the urgent instead of reveling in the joy of their own passions.

Could it be that "I hafta do it this way because..." and "I can't do it differently because..." really are hard-wired into the human soul?

Nope. For What Is Your Life's Work? I collected thousands of letters from us to our loved ones. Most letters followed this structure: "Dear Son/Daughter: Don't make the same mistakes I did. I knew what mattered: You and our family. But I kept making the same excuse: that my boss's bosses' demands were more urgent. Don't do that. Have the courage to follow your dreams. Have the courage to say 'No' more often, and say 'Yes' to what's inside of you."

## BILL JENSEN

*Bill Jensen is an expert on work complexity and cutting through clutter to what really matters. His first book,* Simplicity, *remains a best-seller. His latest,* Hacking Work: Breaking Stupid Rules for Smart Results, *reveals an underground army of benevolent hackers—breaking all sorts of rules so everyone can do great work. Follow Bill on Twitter at @simpletonbill and on the Web at SimplerWork.com.*

*Hacking work is getting the system to work for you; it's making it easier for you to do great work.*

Most of us would like our eulogy to read "She followed her bliss," but instead we live a life of "She never missed a meeting, no matter how wasteful it was."

Stop this! Now!

OK, but how?

I'm asked that by most every manager I meet. From Mr. Simplicity, they expect a checklist. I try to comply. I build what matters into how to write better emails, run better meetings, build better strategies. But I also try to help those managers discover that those are just Trojan horse to-do's. As we discuss each one, I'm sneaking in something much more valuable.

The real answer is always introspection—to draw upon something inside yourself that forces you to keep remembering, "This is what really matters," and to constantly build that into your daily actions.

For me, it was the death of my mom. For you, it may be realizing how many hours of your child's life you've missed, or how often your passions fell to the bottom of the list. Whatever it is, it's inside of you, it's not in any checklist, and it certainly doesn't come from any outsider—your manager, your mentor, or me.

Reach inside yourself. You already know how to close the biggest distance in the world. If you just needed a nudge, then let this be it.

If you'd still like a to-do, here it is: Hack your work. Bypass all that stupid stuff by hacking workarounds. (Benevolently, of course.)

Business is broken and it needs your help. For decades, business has offloaded too much work onto you by being completely corporate-centered in how it built tools, processes, and procedures—ensuring your company's success, but not necessarily yours.

That is changing. Empowering tools that were once the domain of our employers are now available for free or next-to-nothing—downloadable to your smartphone. And a new generation is entering the workforce knowing how to use these tools to ensure their success while delivering what their company needs. (That's the benevolent part.)

Your choice is no longer: "Deal with the crap or don't... and risk your job." Benevolent hackers take the usual ways of doing things and bypass them to produce improved results. These are White Hat hackers, performing workarounds for companies that are too slow or bureaucratic to make much-needed changes.

You could be one of these hackers. Hacking work is getting the system to work for you, not just the other way around; it's making it easier for you to do great work.

Every day in every workplace, hackers are the heroes who ensure that business succeeds despite itself. Their innovations plug the holes in business's strategies, structures, tools, and processes with workarounds.

Want to make more of a difference, doing more of what matters? Hack some stupid work today.

## AVOIDING SUCK-NESS AND SILENCE

When I was an admin at Apple, I used to go to meetings and see the problems so clearly, when others could not. I didn't think I had the right or the capabilities to speak the truth. I worried about being seen as too low in rank, too young, or too brown, or too female, or too uneducated to offer the solution to the group.

But mostly, I worried about being too wrong.

So, I kept quiet and learned to sit on my hands lest they rise up and betray me. I would rather keep my job, by staying within the lines, than say something and risk looking stupid.

Now, twenty years later, as I see companies trying to figure out their tough problems—like which new markets to go into, or how to create the next-generation products, or how to defend against a big-ass competitor—I see a similar pattern occurring.

The thing that stops any of these good teams from being as successful as they might is not stupidity. The issue is rarely stupid people. Rather, what limits success, growth, and winning is something more akin to silence.

Perhaps you can see how this happens where you work.

Perhaps you were attending a new strategy rollout and you knew that big chunks of it wouldn't work. Or the latest re-org focuses on optimizing the delivery of X, when you know the market is really looking for Y. Or your leader never seems to address the one thing that is stopping a bunch of other things from being successful.

## NILOFER MERCHANT

*Nilofer Merchant is a noted CEO, Fortune 500 leader, published author, and behavioral strategist. She has a reputation for enabling companies to win, if not dominate, their markets. Her first book,* The New How, *addresses the art of setting strategy so it becomes a reality. Follow Nilofer on Twitter at @nilofer and on the Web at NiloferMerchant.com.*

> *What kills us is not that we've got it wrong, or not quite right. What kills us is that we can't talk about its being wrong.*

Maybe you've heard hallway chatter, like "Don't they get it?" or "Will they ever deal with this?" The thinking goes like this—the plan seems crazy and the issue is Z, but since it's plain to me, well, they must see it, too.

What kills us is not that we've got it wrong, or not quite right. What kills us is that we can't talk about its being wrong.

We conclude that a topic is mysteriously taboo. We tell ourselves that we're too busy or that it's not our issue.

Or maybe we know we really should speak up. But who wants to be a bearer of bad news to the powers that be? What if we're wrong? What if we're mocked? As Lincoln has been known to say, better to keep silent and be thought a fool, than speak up and remove all doubt. And so, in the end, too many times, we choose silence. We don't express our viewpoint and offer what we think could help.

Here's the cost of our silence. When issues stay unaddressed, stagnant, broken, we all fail.

We ship bad products, our brand suffers, and our company performance plummets. In general, things suck. Not just for "them" but for all of "us," too. The cost of silence is suck-ness.

When we are silent, we are hurting the outcome. Minority viewpoints have been proven to aid the quality of decision making in juries, by teams, and for the purpose of innovation. Research proves that even when the different points of view are wrong, they cause people to think better, to create more solutions, and to improve creativity in problem solving.

So here's a way to avoid this suck-ness, a way to both speak your truth and not lose your job.

Don't say, "This is the problem." That blunt approach risks your looking the fool and quite probably pissing someone off.

Rather, ask this:

"Could it be... that this is the problem?"

"Could it be" is a conversation starter, rather than an assertion. It is the way you put an idea out there without having to defend it. "Could it be" allows the issue to be a question for everyone. "Could it be" allows for a dialogue rather than a yes/no argument.

The blind need you to see. The silence needs to be broken. And perhaps risking being the fool is necessary to move forward. Underlying all that is courage—courage to speak, courage to risk, courage to step forward rather than sit quietly. Courage to break the silence. When you do, the blind will see, the different viewpoints will be heard, and we can reduce suck-ness where we work.

Could it be... that you are ready to speak up?

## YOU THE OPERATING SYSTEM

It's almost certain that you are living and working in a context that is increasingly:

Hyper-connected

Always on

Mobile

On-demand

Virtual and interactive

Boundary-less

Information rich

Multi-task oriented

Time constrained

Fast in pace and high in intensity

Clearly there are both benefits and challenges that come with this accelerating rate of technological change. Many of us will regularly upgrade the operating systems on our devices or upgrade the devices themselves to keep pace. It's a smart thing to do because the upgrading of operating systems, devices, and functions delivers great benefits and value in our work and in our lives.

We also have an opportunity to optimize ourselves, to rebalance and calibrate our "personal operating systems"—the ways that we are choosing to live and work—for the benefit of ourselves and others.

## RICH FERNANDEZ

*Rich Fernandez, Ph.D., leads learning and organizational development at eBay. Rich is passionate about personal and organizational excellence, and has worked for nearly two decades in large companies, as well as in hospitals and educational settings, to help create cultures of excellence and possibility.*

*We have an opportunity to optimize ourselves, to rebalance and calibrate our personal operating systems.*

Just as you could not run a very old operating system on your computer and make it function effectively in contemporary life, we have little choice but to find new ways of working, living, and being in order to function effectively in our increasingly complex, dynamic, and technology-rich world.

Recently at eBay we started running experiments to help people in our workplace take more deliberate, thoughtful approaches to how they are living their lives at work and beyond. Specifically, we were interested in addressing concerns about the stress, pressure, and demands that people were feeling. A few core principles informed our approach:

### 1. Positive disruption

First, it is necessary to "positively disrupt" the rhythms and routines that prevent us from living and working optimally—because requests and demands on our time and attention often arrive in an indiscriminate way. It's our responsibility to determine what's important, structure our lives, and work around those priorities and follow through. We encourage people to explore their core values, and we offer them tools for organizing and prioritizing everything from their inboxes to the way they can deliberately structure downtime.

### 2. Cultivating well-being and engagement through deliberate practice

We know that the only way to effect positive changes at the personal, familial, and organizational levels is to help people feel connected to needed changes and develop a sustained, deliberate practice over time. Living well engenders engagement and well-being, both of which are outcomes of a deliberate set of practices. We encourage people (and give them the tools) to take regular breaks, utilize fitness facilities, eat well, exercise flexible work options, and cultivate a regular set of mindfulness practices that promote well-being. Extensive research shows that people who report experiencing well-being and engagement in their daily lives and work are much more healthy, productive, and successful than others. Plus they have more fun!

### 3. Developing a community of practice

A group of people who can provide ongoing support for needed changes is critical—because it is not possible to install new operating practices, rhythms, and routines without the guidance, feedback, and support of others. We offer large-scale programs and peer-led support groups to help people make the positive changes they seek. But everyone has a community they can participate in, and it is critical to have the support of a community, friends, or family to effect desired changes.

Based on these principles and some survey fact-finding, we began offering people in our organization content and programming that focused on personal excellence and well-being. These types of programs give us the tools to install practices in our lives that promote well-being and personal excellence.

It is important to point out here that you don't need to wait for your organization to install programs and content that help you develop practices for improving your well-being and personal excellence. There are several accessible, low-cost tools out there that almost anyone would find useful.

Some recommended resources (that we also use in our organization) are Gallup's Wellness Finder (with online assessment and tracking tools), Values in Action assessments (available through the Authentic

Happiness site at the University of Pennsylvania), the Strengths Essentials suite of tools, and some of the tools and resources offered at The Energy Project.

Most important, we encourage everyone to identify the types of personal actions they can take to thoughtfully manage everyday life—utilizing the principles of positive disruption, deliberate practice, and the support of a community—so that life at work and at home is nothing less than a source of vitality and joy.

## BUILD BRIDGES

For most of human history, long-distance communication was a cumbersome affair. Documents had to be carried on foot or horseback, or in the holds of ships, and they often took weeks or months to arrive at their destination. Then, in 1835, Samuel F.B. Morse invented the telegraph, and the world changed. Suddenly, it was possible to send messages down wires and cables, instantaneously connecting people across great distances.

The rise of the telegraph system was far from seamless, however. The infrastructure took many years to be installed, and users often had to struggle with gaps in the network. One of the most maddening of those gaps lay in the heart of Europe. The Belgian line terminated in Brussels, while the German line went only as far as Aachen. Messages had to be transcribed and carried overland across the 77 miles separating the two cities.

But one small company saw a business opportunity in this problem. In 1849, this company bought a flock of carrier pigeons and used them to fly messages between Brussels and Aachen, dramatically reducing transit times. Within a few years, the company had grown to become one of the leading telegraph agencies. Its name was Reuters.

There's an important lesson here: When a disruptive new technology arrives, the greatest business opportunities often lie not in creating the disruption but in mending it—in figuring out, as Reuters did, a way to use an older, established technology as a bridge to carry customers to the benefits of the emerging technology.

When we talk about business innovation today, we tend to use terms like "breakthrough" and "pioneering" and "revolutionary." But some

## NICHOLAS CARR

*Nicholas Carr writes about technology, culture, and economics and is the author of the best-selling books* The Shallows: What the Internet Is Doing to our Brains *and* The Big Switch. *Follow Nicholas on the Web at RoughType.com.*

*Some of the greatest and most lucrative innovations are essentially conservative, providing a bridge between past and future.*

of the greatest and most lucrative innovations are essentially conservative, providing a bridge between past and future. They are brought to market by companies that are as adept at looking backward as they are at looking forward and that have the skill and patience to achieve the most commercially attractive balance between the old and the new.

Bridge-building is a powerful strategy for a simple reason: new technologies tend to take hold slowly, advancing through a long series of technical and market barriers. The automatic telephone switch was invented by the end of the nineteenth century, but manual exchanges continued to be widely used for another fifty years. Facsimile transmission also became possible in the late 1800s, but it took a century for it to become commonplace. Consumer PCs were introduced in 1975, but by 2000 only half of U.S. households owned one.

The future, in other words, arrives in fits and starts. There are several reasons why this is so. A new technology may be difficult to use, requiring specialized expertise. Or it may be plagued by bugs that reduce its utility. In the early days of railroads, trains had the annoying habit of going off the rails; it was only after wheels, couplings, and tracks had advanced and become standardized that train transport became reliable enough to be broadly adopted. Or, as with the telegraph, a new technology may involve the building of a physical infrastructure, requiring a lot of money and time.

Sometimes progress goes slowly not because of flaws in the technology, but because consumers resist its adoption. Early versions of new technologies are often prohibitively expensive, for example, and that can restrict their use to a small slice of the market for years. In other cases, buying a new technology requires abandoning an old and familiar one, something consumers are rarely eager to do. Years after color televisions had been introduced, many people continued to happily use their old black-and-white sets. Mobile telephony was embraced slowly in the United States because the country's landline network was so reliable. Who needed a cell phone?

Companies rarely see these roadblocks clearly. In business, after all, innovation is spearheaded by enthusiasts—product developers, marketers, entrepreneurs—who tend to be much more enamored of new technologies than are run-of-the-mill consumers. The innovators' desire to be pioneers—to do cool things fast—blinds them to the more mundane realities of the marketplace. As a result, companies can easily fall into a trap: They can rush headlong into the future only to find that no market yet exists.

Thinking in terms of bridges rather than breakthroughs can help you avoid such mistakes. Clear a path into the future for customers, and you just may find that they'll follow you anywhere.

*Wanting to do two non-compatible things has a name. It's called stress.*

## HEADS OR TAILS?

It's come down to a very simple question, actually, one with only two answers.

Are you racing to the top or racing to the bottom?

Are you going to become ever more compliant, ever better at fitting in, or are you prepared to commit to standing out and following your own map? Can't do both.

The economy is calling names, and you need to either stand up or sit down. All the rest is commentary.

The confusion I see online is caused by people who want both. They want the apparent safety of following the herd (doing the safe thing), while they also gain the head start (and the joy) of carving their own niche.

Wanting to do two non-compatible things has a name. It's called stress.

So, decide.

Even better, write it down. Commit. Tell your family. Live it. All the way or none of the way.

## SETH GODIN

*Seth Godin has written many books, all best-sellers, and is the founder of The Domino Project. His blog on marketing, respect, and how ideas spread is one of the most read in the world. Follow Seth on the Web at sethgodin.typepad.com or on Twitter at @thisissethsblog.*

# TAKE SMALL STEPS

*"Always do whatever's next."*

George Carlin,
Comedian and philosopher

One of the great experiences of the world is to walk on top of the Sydney Harbour Bridge. You don gray overalls and a hard hat, and then climb up and up until at last you're standing over one of the great cities of the world, with the harbor stretching away before you, leading toward the Heads and the Pacific Ocean.

When Paul Cave first conceived of the idea of such a walk, he was presented with a long list of reasons that it wouldn't work—hundreds of objections related to safety, logistics, heritage, and conservation issues. The sensible thing would have been to have stopped right there. But he didn't. Rather, for nine years he systematically overcame each objection, point by point, step by step. In 1998, BridgeClimb was finally launched, and it has become one of Australia's most successful tourist experiences.

## IN THIS SECTION

## ORDINARY COURAGE

In any leadership role worth having, you're often called upon to make all kinds of courageous decisions. Are our organization's ethics in order? Is a corporate bully unfairly sidelining good ideas from underlings? Does a competitor need to be called out for going too far?

We often think of courage as a display of bravery in the face of entrenched, often external, opposition. When situations like those arise, I hope you'll make decisions in a courageous way that helps you look back with pride.

But if you want to slay another dragon, look at the one in the mirror. The truly courageous know that courage is most significant when you are facing your own weaknesses. You've probably heard that you should focus on your strengths, and that's usually a good idea—but you also can't proceed blindly ahead, pretending you have no weaknesses. Instead, show courage by being willing to change yourself.

How do you do that? Start with these ideas:

### Conduct an honest self-assessment
If you think about it, you're probably well aware of at least one area you need to make adjustments in. It's probably something you've been putting off or otherwise avoiding. Show courage by finding a way to compensate for the weakness.

### Ask for help
Make it clear to everyone you work with that you want to slay your own dragons. You probably know what they are, but if not, colleagues

## CHRIS GUILLEBEAU

*Chris Guillebeau has been challenging authority since 1978, with the mission to help people take the road less traveled. His most recent book is* The Art of Non-Conformity. *Follow Chris on Twitter at @chrisguillebeau and on the Web at ChrisGuillebeau.com.*

*The truly courageous know that courage is most significant when you are facing your own weaknesses.*

will tell you when they know you're serious about their input. (Be sure to get input from peers, subordinates, and bosses.)

## Take immediate steps

Don't make a thirty-step plan; make a two-step plan: think about it and do something about it. Ask for advice on a crazy idea. Contribute more—or less—at a meeting. Make a list of a dozen colleagues; then think of one specific thing you can do to help each of them this week. If you get off track somewhere, apologize quickly and publicly.

Stand up and speak up for all that is good, but also stand up to yourself.

Choose ordinary courage today.

## DANCING WITH UNCERTAINTY

At around 2 p.m., the meeting ended and there I stood. Committed. I'd signed a six-year lease on a floor in a building in Hell's Kitchen, NY. I was married, with a three-month-old little girl and a home. The plan was to open what I hoped would become New York City's top-rated yoga studio.

But there was a problem. I had no reputation in the yoga world, no experience in the yoga business or teaching world, no relationships, and, according to many, no business opening a studio.

Oh, one more thing. The date I signed the lease: September 10, 2001.

The next morning, my world came crashing down. Two planes hit the towers, friends were lost, and there I sat with a freshly minted six-year lease to launch a business in a city that was both in flames and in mourning.

The logical thing, the safe option, would have been to fold the newly formed corporation and walk away. But I couldn't. If this was the thing I had to do before, it had now become the thing my city needed more than anything. The thing I needed.

People were wandering the streets in a daze, looking for something to do, some way to help, a place to find solace, community. The pain was still there, profoundly magnified and expanded. The air was thick with uncertainty and fear. I had to push forward. This was not a time for numbers or logic; it was a time for intuition and instinct. No spreadsheet could support what I was about to do.

If the pivotal moments of creation were easy or rational, everyone would make the choice to push forward. But most people don't

## JONATHAN FIELDS

*Jonathan Fields is an entrepreneur, author, and speaker. His latest book is* Uncertainty: Turning Fear and Doubt Into Fuel for Brilliance, *and he writes about innovation, entrepreneurship, legacy, and meaning. Follow Jonathan on Twitter at @jonathanfields and on the Web at JonathanFields.com, and see him speak as part of the TEDx series.*

*Not knowing how it will end and whether you'll be able to pull it off is a mandatory part of the process.*

because it makes them uncomfortable. Uncertainty isn't an innately fun emotion, but the ability to become more comfortable with it and even embrace it over time is mission-critical in the quest to create anything that matters. So, I leaned in.

From that willingness to dance with the unknown, a series of events and decisions unfolded that led to the launch of an incredible adventure. Three years in, with a driven team in place, we were named the top center in NYC, and we grew into one of the largest teacher training schools on the East Coast. Tens of thousands of people found peace, stillness, friends, freedom, and community.

Anything worth doing, whether a corporate initiative, a personal quest, or an entrepreneurial endeavor, will be filled with uncertainty. Not knowing how it will end, whether you'll be able to pull it off, or what it will look or feel like when you do, is a mandatory part of the process, at least in the early phase.

Over time, leaps of faith will be replaced by information. Fear and anxiety will cede to shape, form, certainty, and comfort. But if you try to rush the process or shut it down because you can't handle the uncertainty, fear, and risk, you effectively shut down your genius creation engine.

So why not do the opposite? Rather than trying to snuff out uncertainty and fear and taking down your endeavor along with them, honor their role as signposts of innovation, and find ways to be able to embrace those seeming demons.

When you learn to dance with uncertainty, the doors to genius swing open.

## STOP COMPLAINING AND MUSTER THE COURAGE TO LEAD

I want to apologize at the outset for opening with words that might sound harsh. I know you have a lot going on. You have a team to supervise, deadlines to meet, projects for which you are responsible, reports to complete, numbers to achieve, meetings to attend, an uncertain economy to face, and your health and family obligations beside. Work can often seem a lot more like being caught in an avalanche than like spending a day on the ski slopes.

Even so, I feel compelled to say: stop complaining and start leading.

There… I said it. I firmly believe that the courage to act is one of the best ways to re-engage with your work and overcome the natural propensity to focus on all that might be going wrong.

Humans are hard-wired to see risk and be vigilant for problems. We have stress responses that help enable us to deal with difficulties. Fear actually helps to protect us from taking outrageous risks, and it prepares us, physiologically, for fight or flight. In the 9-to-5 world of business, anxiety pushes us to rise to the occasion by working harder at the eleventh hour and prevents us from taking outlandish gambles. A certain amount of caution is smart. This natural attention to what might go wrong is what helps executives and other leaders take stock of competition, predict unfavorable economic and marketplace trends, and identify internal organizational deficits. The downside of this psychological protective mechanism is that it can lead us to be too problem-focused and too cautious in our behaviors.

The antidote to too much prudence is courage. When most people think of courage they imagine soldiers fighting in a war or emergency personnel saving people from burning buildings. While these

## DR. ROBERT BISWAS-DIENER

*Dr. Robert Biswas-Diener is widely known as the Indiana Jones of Positive Psychology because his research on happiness has taken him to such far-flung places as Greenland, India, and Kenya. He is a part-time instructor at Portland State University and sits on the editorial boards of the Journal of Happiness Studies and Journal of Positive Psychology. Robert is the author of* Practicing Positive Psychology Coaching *and co-author, with Ben Dean, of* Positive Psychology Coaching. *Follow Robert on Twitter at @biswasdiener and on the Web at PositiveAcorn.com.*

*Stop complaining and start leading.*

physical actions are undoubtedly acts of courage, I believe the phenomenon is a bit more commonplace.

Courage is simply acting in a way that puts you at risk in a fearful or uncomfortable situation in which the outcome is uncertain. Sticking up for an underdog at a team meeting is an act of courage. Launching a new product is an act of courage. Confronting a supervisor on a point of disagreement is an act of courage. These are examples of the "willingness to act" even in situations in which there could be costs and in which complaining and idleness are far easier.

Anyone in a leadership role, however, is called upon to inspire others, in part, through his or her ability to act even under tough circumstances. That is, to be courageous. This is more than an opinion of mine; it is part of the job description. In fact, research by Cooper Woodard suggests that executives experience less fear and show a greater willingness to act than do college students, police and fire personnel, and members of the Reserve Officer Training Corps (ROTC)! You will, in essence, be at your best when you are rising to the occasion of handling work difficulties and not when you are griping about them at the water cooler.

How can you be more courageous? How can you up the ante on your courage quotient and be more willing to act? I have interviewed dozens of people who are naturally high in courage—high-powered lawyers, small-business entrepreneurs, HR professionals, and executives—and they point to a number of personal practices that help them—as one woman put it—step through fear.

First, understand that your approach to work overload and other tough situations is a matter of attitude. Complaints about what is wrong can be replaced with the question "how am I (or how are we) going to get through this?" This leads directly to a solutions-focused mindset that is more pleasant, engaging, and capacity building.

Next, appreciate the fact that work stress is real and legitimate. Doing so can help by focusing you on strategies for dealing with stress, such as getting regular physical exercise, and away from the possibility of beating yourself up over occasional low performance or anything that appears to be less than perfection.

Third, seek social support: we humans are at our best when we work in coordinated and supportive groups, and this is certainly true of organizations. Get constructive 360-degree feedback, seek out a role model or mentor, and celebrate even the small successes. Research is clear in suggesting that praise and social celebration are important factors in engagement on the job.

Finally, you can pump up your courage quotient by using any trick that will help you face an uncertain future. A silly, but powerful, means to do this is to use a talisman, or "lucky charm," that helps you act a bit more boldly than you otherwise might. This talisman might be a religious symbol, a pair of lucky socks or underwear, a photo on your desk, a favorite watch, or almost any other item that symbolizes strength for you. In the end, those teams and projects and deadlines are just begging for you to rise to the occasion.

## CHANGE YOUR CAREER WHILE AT WORK TODAY

If you're jonesing for a new career, you're not alone.

A surprising statistic from Robert Half International's Employment Dynamics and Growth Expectations (EDGE) Report revealed that more than half of employees plan to make a career change or go back to school.

Given those aspirations, you might want to take steps now—while you still have a paying job—to make your future transition easier. Here are a few tips for incorporating the career-change process into your daily routine:

### When you wake up

When your alarm goes off, grab a journal and a pen and take ten minutes to consider what you like and what you don't like in a work environment. Thought-starter questions include:

- What is important to you and what are your values?
- What is your definition of success?
- How do you prefer to work?
- What type of job would make you want to sit in traffic for hours just for the privilege of showing up?

### While drinking your morning coffee

Instead of surfing Facebook, check out the Bureau of Labor Statistics' Occupational Outlook Handbook. Browse through the hundreds of thousands of occupations and make a note of the ones that interest you. Jot down the transferable skills required (i.e., project management, sales, marketing, finance), and as you're going through your day, think about how you may already be using those skills in your current job.

## ALEXANDRA LEVIT

*Alexandra Levit is a business, workplace, and career author, consultant, and speaker. She's the author of the forthcoming book* Blind Spots: 10 Business Myths You Can't Afford to Believe on Your New Path to Success. *Follow Alexandra on Twitter at @alevit and on the Web at AlexandraLevit.com.*

*If you're jonesing for a new career, you're not alone.*

### Over lunch

Search for organizations on LinkedIn.com that do the kind of work you're interested in. Use this site, as well as resources like your college career center or alumni network, to connect with individuals currently working in your target fields. Email them and request a half-hour informational interview in which you ask specific questions about training requirements, responsibilities, salary, work environment, and opportunities for advancement. As long as you are polite, no one will fault you for wanting the real scoop.

### Before you leave work

When you're finished with your daily duties, stay after-hours and check out an online course designed to help you facilitate a career change. Online video presentations often provide the same value as more expensive, time-consuming, and difficult-to-travel-to seminars.

### On the train home

Many people resist changing careers because they feel like they can't afford it. Start creating a nest egg for your transition now by creating a spreadsheet on your smartphone to keep track of where your money is going on a daily basis. If you do this on the train for a month or even just for a few weeks, you'll be amazed at the data you'll accumulate.

You'll start to see patterns of unnecessary spending (your morning Starbucks run, sushi takeout, etc.) and areas where you can tighten your belt. A great question to ask yourself is: "Do I really need this?" If you honestly don't, then put the money away for your career change.

## COUNTDOWN TO ESCAPE VELOCITY

Are you finding your pay not stretching? Do you know someone who has been out of work for more than their share of time? Are you in an area that has been hit by economic disaster after disaster?

Or even simpler, are you just tired of the job you have, and hoping to move to something else?

I've been thinking about escape velocity since the beginning of 2010. In scientific terms, escape velocity is the speed one needs to attain to leave the gravitational pull of a planet. It seems like the perfect way to explain that time when we're stuck in a behavior or a situation and can't yet pull free to move to a new, better thing. Escape velocity, to me, is that effort you put in to shift from the bad situation to the better situation before you're able to make the big move.

It doesn't have to be about work. If you're thirty pounds overweight, you might start escaping your previous lifestyle and choices by improving little bits of your health and fitness. Essentially, the idea of escape velocity is realizing that you want to move to something better for yourself or your family and knowing that you need to make some changes.

Here's an example from my life: I had a job just like anyone. And then I switched into a new career, where things were much less steady. We went into debt. We started living a bit more chaotically. And I found myself without enough money to pay the mortgage from time to time. It was a raw spot to be in, and I found that I needed to figure something out or I'd go down completely.

## CHRIS BROGAN

*Chris Brogan is the President of Human Business Works, an online education and community company for small businesses and solo entrepreneurs. He also consults for blue-chip organizations on the future of business communications and social software technologies. He is, with Julian Smith, the co-author of* Trust Agents: Using the Web to Build Influence, Improve Reputation, and Earn Trust. *Follow Chris on Twitter at @chrisbrogan and on the Web at ChrisBrogan.com.*

I started small. I started asking myself, "What else could I do to earn some money above and beyond my salary?" I started looking around at how other people were making money. I took inventory on what I knew how to do. When I boiled it all down, I was able to find a few things to bring in the money we needed.

Here's the countdown to reaching your own escape velocity:

10. Acknowledge that you're not happy with some situation in your life. Name that.

9. Decide what you want the next situation to be. Name that.

8. Add some detail to that: instead of "lose thirty pounds" or "make more money," decide that you want to work out four times a week or that you want to earn another $1500 a month. Whatever you need it to be.

7. Decide what you know how to do.

6. Decide whom you know how to reach.

5. Determine if the things you can do are useful to the folks you can reach.

4. Determine whether there's an opportunity there.

3. If the goal is more of a self-improvement goal, figure out who can partner with you for accountability.

2. Make sure you have finite goals but also a broader vision.

1. Think small, and think in chunks. If you need another $12K a year to make ends meet, that's only $1K a month, which is only $250 a week. See?

*Push past the gravitational pull of what isn't working.*

You can get there. It just takes passion, commitment, and a vision. I say "just" as if that's easy. It's not. But escape velocity is about that very moment of pushing past the gravitational pull of what isn't working.

That's worth it, right?

## "INDECISIVE LEADER" IS AN OXYMORON

Have you ever had to swerve your car to miss a squirrel in the road? I've had a ton of near-misses in my time, mostly because Mr. Squirrel ran out of nowhere into the middle of the road, got freaked out, and darted back to one side, then the other, then back to the middle— everywhere but off the road! The problem? The little guy got scared, and in his fear, he couldn't decide which way to go. He couldn't make a decision, and ... blump, blump. Ouch.

I've seen a lot of business leaders do the same thing. They find themselves trapped in a busy intersection or a complicated merger or a tense personnel issue or a heated debate with partners, and they just freeze. They get overwhelmed with all the options and all the variables, and something in them totally locks up. The Bible says, "A double-minded man is unstable in all his ways." I call that idea "squirrel theology."

Like a squirrel on the freeway, these leaders are paralyzed by fear. What if I screw up? What if I make the wrong decision? What if someone is hurt by what I decide? What if this costs us more money? What if the next deal will be better? What if, what if, what if?

Your business, your family, your team, and your future are all paralyzed when you are. If you are in charge, then it all starts and stops with you. You set the pace; you set the tone. You'll never hit your target if all you ever say is, "Ready, aim, aim, aim, aim, aim." At some point, you've got to pull the trigger. If you don't, you put everything you've worked for—everything you've dreamed of—in jeopardy. You're like a guy who dates a lady for twenty years but never pops the question. At some point, she's going to leave you for someone who will commit. Your team and your business will do the same.

## DAVE RAMSEY

*Dave Ramsey is America's trusted voice on money and business. He's written three* New York Times *best-selling books:* Financial Peace, More Than Enough, *and* The Total Money Makeover. *His latest book,* EntreLeadership, *will be released in September, 2011. The Dave Ramsey Show is heard by millions of listeners each week on hundreds of radio stations. Follow Dave on Twitter at @DaveRamsey and on the Web at daveramsey.com.*

I'm speaking from experience here. After several years in business, I finally figured out that fear was the root of all of my indecision. Every time I found myself going back and forth for hours and days and weeks on a decision, I traced it back to some specific fear. Once I realized what was going on, making decisions got a lot easier.

Now my company has as one of its core operating principles this little statement: "We don't make decisions based on fear." If we're up against a wall, we say it out loud. We'll say, "I'm afraid that...." Once it's out there, we can deal with it. We can talk about it and pray about it. It's like Dorothy Bernard once said: "Courage is just fear that has said its prayers."

That doesn't mean we don't get scared. We do. We're fighting giants all day every day, taking on huge industries that would love to put us out of business. But we never let that paralyze us or prevent us from moving forward. If we let the spirit of fear dominate our decisions, then every competitor and every obstacle would send us running to the corner, sucking our thumbs. It's wise to take an honest look at the threats, criticisms, and outright insults that others may hurl at you, but it's unwise to give them the power to bring your business to a screeching halt.

The bottom line is that leadership is hard; it's not for wimps. If you want to lead, you've got to fight. You've got to dig in your heels, put your back into the work, and push your business or family or personal goals forward. Squirrels freeze. Leaders lead. Be a leader.

*The bottom line is that leadership is hard; it's not for wimps.*

## CREATE A PERSONAL MASTER PLAN

Want to experience immediate clarity about your life and work? Want to ensure that you're prioritizing the projects that will lead to the results you desire most?

Create a personal master plan.

### Step #1: The mind dump
Here's what to do first: grab a pen and five sheets of paper. At the top of the first page, boldly scribble "Here's What I Want…"

Now go nuts.

List all of your big dreams, major projects, and minor preferences. Anything you want is fair game—what other people want you to want doesn't really matter. Try to self-censor as little as possible—things that other people wouldn't find socially acceptable are okay, too. (You can always burn the list later if you're worried that someone will read it.)

Dump the contents of your mind onto paper as completely as possible. You'll know you're done when you can't think of anything else you might possibly want.

### Step #2: Sorting
Here's the second step: we're going to sort the list you created into three separate lists to add a bit of clarity about what each item actually is. Here are the categories:

## JOSH KAUFMAN

*Josh Kaufman is an independent business professor who is committed to helping people master the essentials of business practice. He is the author of* The Personal MBA: Master the Art of Business. *Follow Josh on Twitter at @joshkaufman and on the Web at personalmba.com.*

1. Goals—statements of achievement. Well-formed goals pass what I call the "Everest Test"—if you want to climb Mt. Everest, you know precisely when you've accomplished your goal. The best goals are positive, immediate, concrete, and specific. They're also things that you have the power to accomplish if you invest enough time and effort.

2. States of being—the qualities of your present experience. "I want to be happy" is not a goal, since you can feel happy in one moment and miserable in the next. States of being are actually decision criteria, not goals. If you "want to feel free," and you're not feeling free in a given moment, you know you need to change something.

3. Habits—daily supporting behaviors that keep you healthy, calm, and sane. Habits take some willpower to install, but the results accumulate over time. Brushing your teeth is a habit. So is going for a walk every day after dinner.

*Prioritization is actually the process of deciding what's not important: what you're not going to focus on right now.*

### Step #3: Prioritizing

Once you've separated your first list into these three lists, you're ready for the third stage: prioritizing.

Most people think of prioritization as "deciding what's most important." The trouble with that definition is that it easily leads to feeling overwhelmed—way too many things feel important at once. (If it wasn't important, it wouldn't be on your list.)

That why it's easy to feel overworked and stressed out: unless you make a conscious choice, your mind will continue to want everything, all at once.

Prioritization is actually the process of deciding what's not important: what you're not going to focus on right now. If you delete, delegate, or defer your less important wants, you free up time and energy for the remainder, which are more important by definition.

Start with your Goals list, and apply a simple rule: assume you can accomplish only 50 percent of the items on this list this year. Which items do you keep, and which do you cross off your list? Cut your list in half.

When you're done cutting, cut the list in half again, then again, until you have four items left. Those are your most important goals right now.

When you've finished pruning your Goals, do the same for your States of Being and Habits lists. Yes, the last few cuts are the most difficult, but they're also the most valuable.

Cutting something from your list doesn't mean you're giving up on it completely—it simply means that it's less important than other items right now. Everything you cut can go on what David Allen calls a "Someday/Maybe" list, which you can revisit later, when you're ready for a new challenge.

## Using your master plan

Creating a master plan takes at least an hour, but it'll be one of the most productive hours you spend this year. Here's why: having a master plan makes it very easy to determine your most important tasks each day.

At the beginning of each day, review your master plan. Figure out the very next thing you can do to achieve each of your goals. Those tasks will, by definition, lead most directly to what you want, so do them first. Remind yourself of how you want to experience your daily life. Schedule time for the habits that support you.

It's amazing how much a simple list can help you feel grounded, focused, and motivated each day.

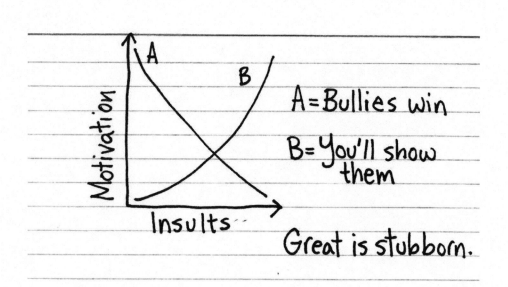

A = Bullies win

B = You'll show them

Great is stubborn.

# RESILIENCE

*In the past decade, several African countries have cut malaria deaths by more than half—but we're determined to bring that number down to near zero.*

# EMBRACE SYSTEMS

*"Arrange whatever pieces come your way."*

Virginia Woolf,
Author

Bill Bryson's book *A Short History of Nearly Everything* is extraordinary. It makes science accessible and funny, and it makes it clear that it's nothing short of extraordinary that we're able to exist as we are on this planet.

That existence is in no small part due to the successful systems that surround us. Here's just one example—the moon.

Our moon is substantially bigger than any other moon in the solar system. As well as causing tides and transforming men into werewolves, the moon's gravitational weight keeps our planet's axis stable. That's handy, because it means that with a stable axis we're able to have seasons. And having regular seasons allows us to cultivate food, which in many ways is the very basis of civilization.

People can rail against systems. And true, when they're bad, they're really bad. But the opposite of a bad system isn't chaos. It's a good system, and the contributors here show you the value of that.

# IN THIS SECTION

David Allen, *The Strategic Value of Clear Space*

Dan Pink, *What's the Matter with Millennials?*

Richard E. Lapchick, *Good Work: Hoops Triumps in Senegal*

Gopi Kallayil, *Flourishing Inside the Lion's Den*

Melissa Daimler, *Learning in the New World of Work*

Les McKeown, *The Power of the Mundane*

Scott Belsky, *Reconsider Your Approach to Organization*

## THE STRATEGIC VALUE OF CLEAR SPACE

How easily you can make a mess is how truly productive you can be. Maximum freedom to generate and play around in creative chaos is the optimal condition for constructive thinking and work.

This is true on a project, in the kitchen, in your office, and at your writing table—anywhere and anytime you want to get real work done.

I don't usually work in a neat fashion. Whether I'm writing an essay, arranging flowers, or making guacamole, I wind up strewing stuff all over the place. If you were to walk into my office while I was working or thinking about something, you'd likely see notes, books, and files strewn around somewhat randomly; a mind-map on my computer screen; and doodles and words scrawled on my whiteboard. When I really get involved in something and my creative juices start flowing, it's likely to look like something exploded in the middle of it. I have a singular focus, but the process doesn't seem orderly until it's done. My best work happens that way. Yours will too.

But if you're already in a mess, you're not free to make one. If you have a desk piled with unfinished, unclear work; if you're trying to repair something in your garage with tools and incomplete projects strewn everywhere; if you've got a thousand unprocessed emails on your computer; or if you've just got a lot of issues and situations on your mind, you're going to be laboring under a serious handicap.

That's why, when I'm not doing anything else, I'm cleaning up. I'm getting my in-basket to zero, getting my desk in order, clearing off the kitchen counter. I'm also capturing, clarifying, and organizing stuff that's pulling on my attention. There's an event, a problem, an

## DAVID ALLEN

*David Allen is one of the modern gurus of personal and organizational productivity. His book* Getting Things Done: The Art of Stress-Free Productivity *is a classic. Follow David on Twitter at @gtdguy and on the Web at DavidCo.com.*

*If you have a problem to solve,*
*limited resources to allocate,*
*or an ambiguous situation to*
*clarify, you'll want to work*
*from a clear deck.*

opportunity coming toward me that I can't see yet. Something will emerge that I will need to focus and work on, coming from the outside or from my own inspiration. When that happens, I want to be ready. Things will get messy, but they will neither start nor end that way.

To tackle something most productively, you must begin in clear space. Physically you need all your tools in order, plus an open table for spreading your raw elements and assembling structures. Psychically you need an empty head, clear of distractions and unfinished business holding your attention hostage. From this starting point you will have your best chances for creative thinking, optimal ability to deal with surprise, and maximum flexibility to come up with work-arounds and innovative solutions. You'll be able to take advantage of serendipitous, potentially valuable ideas.

If you have a problem to solve, limited resources to allocate, or an ambiguous situation to clarify, you'll want to work from a clear deck. You are most productive when all of your available resources are present and accounted for, with an ability to apply relaxed but concentrated focus, and unencumbered by irrelevant pressures and dross.

Zen practices refer to a "beginner's mind." The ready state for enlightenment is a consciousness devoid of preconceptions. Much of the training in the esoteric spiritual disciplines is concerned with de-conditioning the psyche, allowing the full experience and awareness of what's fundamentally true in the present, without the illusory colorings brought on by interpretations from the past or projections into the future.

That's the best place to come from—mentally, emotionally, and psychologically—if you're developing the agenda for the staff meeting, formulating the best way to approach your boss about the delay in a major project, restructuring your board of directors, or planning the family vacation.

This is not a state from which most people live and work.

So, how do you get to that clear place? Can you achieve it only by dedicating years to disciplined asceticism on a Tibetan mountaintop? That's one way, but there's a nice shortcut.

In your physical space, it's pretty simple—just put stuff where it belongs.

In your psychic space, it's also pretty simple (though often quite subtle): you merely have to find out why things are on your mind, and eliminate the cause.

Why are you distracted? What causes your mind to be unclear and inappropriately filled with unproductive thinking that makes no progress on what you're focused on but which creates stress and disturbance that undermines your energy and focus? The basic cause is some decision you haven't yet made and/or the fact that you haven't parked the resulting contents in a trusted system.

"Mom" will be on your mind only if there's something currently going on in your relationship with her (her birthday? her health issue?), about which you haven't clarified what outcome, exactly, you're committed to achieve or what you're specifically going to do about it as a next step to making that happen. And even if you've already clarified those points precisely, if you haven't put the reminders of that outcome and that action step in places you know you will review at the right time, you'll still have "Mom" impinging on your consciousness.

That's going to be equally true about your son's college choice, the status of your retirement account, your choice about hiring a new executive assistant, and your company's strategic direction.

Decide the outcomes you're committed to.

Decide the next physical, visible actions required to move toward them.

Place reminders of all of that where you know you'll look at the right time.

Keep everything in your life and work that way—clear, current, and complete. Discover the strategic value of clear space. Get ready to make a mess.

## WHAT'S THE MATTER WITH MILLENNIALS?

Baby Boomer managers have been asking that question since this cohort of workers—women and men born between the late 1970s and mid-1990s—began streaming into offices several years ago.

Sure, these youngsters are confident. Some of them even work hard. But—let's face it—they're pests.

"They're driving me crazy," forty-something Jack might say to fifty-something Jill. "Every time they complete even the smallest task, they turn around and ask me: 'How was that?' or 'How'd I do?' or 'What'd you think?' I can't take it!"

Jill will nod sympathetically in response. And so might you—if, like me, you're north of age forty.

Many of us interpret our younger colleagues' badgering as some sort of deep-seated emotional neediness—the legacy of cushy childhoods in which, at breakfast each morning, their parents fed them heaping bowls of self-esteem.

Alas—and it pains me slightly to admit this—I think we've got it wrong. The question we should be asking isn't "What's the matter with Millennials?" Instead, we ought to ask: "What's the matter with the workplace?"

Consider a typical twenty-eight-year-old. From the moment she was born, her world has been rich in feedback. When she presses a button, something happens. When she plays a videogame, she gets a score. When she sends a text message, she hears a sound confirming that the message went out. She's lived her whole life on a landscape

## DANIEL H. PINK

*Daniel H. Pink is the author of four provocative books about the changing world of work, including his most recent,* Drive: The Surprising Truth About What Motivates Us. *Follow Dan on Twitter at @danielpink, and on the Web at DanPink.com. This article originally appeared in* The Sunday Telegraph.

*The workplace is one of the most feedback-deprived places in modern life.*

lush with feedback. Yet when she steps through the office door, she finds herself in a veritable feedback desert.

The main—often the only—mechanism for giving her information on how she's doing on the job is the annual performance review. This sturdy feature of organizational life is deeply flawed in at least two ways.

First, it's annual. It's hard to get better at something if you receive feedback on your performance just once a year. Think about Rafael Nadal. His job happens to be to hit tennis balls back and forth across a court. Now imagine if Nadal played tennis for an entire season—and got feedback on his performance only once a year, in a 45-minute meeting with his boss. Absurd, right?

Second, performance reviews are rarely authentic conversations. More often, they are the West's form of kabuki theater—highly stylized rituals in which people recite predictable lines in a formulaic way and hope the experience ends very quickly.

So the problem isn't that the Millennials are wrong. The problem is that they're right. The workplace is one of the most feedback-deprived places in modern life.

Fortunately, it needn't be that way. Let me suggest three modest strategies for greening the desert—and making the workplace a little more feedback-rich.

## 1. Do it yourself

Formal performance appraisals have their place. But we should supplement them with evaluations we do ourselves. Here's how a DIY performance review would work: At the beginning of the month, set out your goals—your performance goals and your learning goals. Then, at the end of the month, call yourself into the office. Where are you making progress? Where are you falling behind? What tools or information do you need to do your job better?

If a conversation with yourself seems odd, try it with a few colleagues. Indeed, many top-performing teams already do this as a matter of course—often without the boss's permission, sometimes without the boss even knowing. This ethic of self-evaluation is also a hallmark of star athletes and great musicians. They set high standards for themselves and then meticulously monitor their own progress.

## 2. Do it through peers

Kimley-Horn, a large American engineering firm, takes a peer-to-peer approach. At this sprawling sixty-office company, anybody at any time can award a colleague a $50 bonus.

Instead of once-a-year acknowledgment from a boss who may not remember your heroic deeds, these modest bonuses allow colleagues to recognize good work instantly—and that, in turn, can create an environment in which feedback more regularly bursts through the dry sands of office life. Last year, Kimley-Horn employees gave each other nearly two thousand of these on-the-spot bonuses.

A person's supervisor must sign off on each award. But ultimately the decision rests with peers, not bosses, and that can make the feedback and recognition more meaningful. As Kimley-Horn's Julie Beauvais puts it, giving employees a way to acknowledge a co-worker "puts the feedback control in the hands of the folks who are closest to the activity."

### 3. Do it with software

Meanwhile, a few entrepreneurial companies have emerged with technological cures for feedback deprivation. Rypple, a startup in Toronto, has developed a suite of social software tools that allow managers and colleagues to provide rich, rapid feedback. For instance, suppose you've been working on a project with fifteen people. At the end of the project, you could use Rypple software to ask your colleagues to suggest areas where you might improve your work. Your fourteen teammates could use the software to respond—anonymously—and to offer real-time advice and guidance.

Rypple co-founder Daniel Debow says he came up with the idea at the previous company he'd launched. He and a partner built a six-hundred-person software company "filled with incredibly talented Millennials. We instituted a traditional performance review process and people hated it, including us." His employees found once-a-year reviews out of synch with their lives. "People kept streaming into our offices looking for coaching, mentoring, and feedback to improve."

So Debow decided that his next company would "foster the 'feedback culture' that Millennials want." His aim—which should be our aim more broadly—was to fix the workplace, not the workers.

## GOOD WORK: HOOPS TRIUMPHS IN SENEGAL

I fell in love with Africa in 1967 when I went to Uganda on the first of my thirty-five trips to the continent. Each time I go, I am amazed by the people and what they are doing.

Last summer, I traveled to Dakar, Senegal, in West Africa, with the NBA's Basketball Without Borders program. I was a guest of the program on this trip, as I was last year when Basketball Without Borders visited South Africa.

The purpose of the Basketball Without Borders program in Africa is to bring together the sixty best young African male players to be trained in basketball skills as well as in life skills, such as leadership, character development, and teamwork, and to involve the players in the community to demonstrate the power of sport to make life better. This year, forty girls were in another camp doing some of the same things as the men.

I had not been to Senegal since the mid-1980s. I remembered it as a nation that beautifully combines French, Arab, and African influences in architecture, art, cuisine, and culture. Senegal has been one of the most stable of the fifty-three independent African nations.

The focus of this Basketball Without Borders trip was on hardcore life-and-death issues, including HIV/AIDS and malaria awareness. The NBA partnered with UNICEF and Nothing But Nets, which distributes mosquito nets and helps residents understand that sleeping under them can save their lives. (Annually, malaria kills a million people across the globe.) Our group of players and coaches spent an afternoon distributing and hanging nets in people's homes.

## RICHARD E. LAPCHICK

*Richard E. Lapchick is the chair of the DeVos Sport Business Management Graduate Program in the College of Business Administration at the University of Central Florida. Lapchick also directs The Institute for Diversity and Ethics in Sport at UCF, is the author of 16 books and the annual* Racial and Gender Report Card, *and is the director of the National Consortium for Academics and Sport. He has joined ESPN.com as a regular commentator on issues of diversity in sport.*

*The focus of this Basketball Without Borders trip was on hardcore life-and-death issues.*

Another afternoon involved a high-energy encounter with perhaps a hundred children at a local YMCA, which the NBA helped modernize and in which the NBA installed fitness training programs. The league supplied the building with a technology center that includes classrooms and more than twenty computers. That YMCA is part of the NBA Cares Legacy Project, which establishes permanent facilities in which children and families can learn and play. It was the twenty-fifth safe haven created by the NBA in Africa.

A huge part of the story from our week in Africa has to be that of an elder son of Senegal. Amadou Fall was born in the country. He came to the U.S. and graduated from the University of the District of Columbia. The President of UDC at that time was Dr. Tilden LeMelle, who had been my African Studies professor when I was completing my Ph.D. two decades earlier. I was the commencement speaker at UDC in the year Adamou graduated. I did not meet him then, but did on the 2009 Basketball Without Borders trip to South Africa. He returned to Senegal as the NBA's vice president for Africa. No other professional sports league has such a position.

Adamou knows what Africa can do. The speeches he gave in Dakar showed that pride and confidence.

The NBA continues to show its commitment to Africa. Amadou Fall is the face of that commitment.

## FLOURISHING INSIDE THE LION'S DEN

People often ask me if Google is the most insanely awesome place to work or if it's like being inside the lion's den.

It's both.

The pace of innovation, the gifted people, and the work environment make it amazing. And at the same time, there's a lot of pressure because of the fast pace, deadlines, meetings, emails, and complexity.

There are certain strategies I've implemented to anchor and ground myself that I'd like to share:

### 1. Optimizing myself

"Optimize Yourself" is a campaign within Google at the moment, and one way to do that is to take advantage of opportunities to learn and grow on an intellectual, emotional, and spiritual level. We have a wide range of experts, like Dr. Oz and Deepak Chopra, come in to teach us, and I seize those opportunities when I can.

### 2. Remembering that you are what you eat

Google believes that your energy level, your performance, and your creativity are functions of what you put inside your body. Google has carefully hired a group of intelligent chefs who think very carefully about what people should be feeding themselves. The chefs make an enormous effort to make sure that a wide range of healthy choices are available, and they're constantly educating Googlers about what to eat, how to choose portion sizes, and what variety you need in your diet.

## GOPI KALLAYIL

*Gopi Kallayil leads Google's AdSense marketing team. He's also a Toastmasters champion and a yoga teacher. See Gopi speak as part of the TEDx series.*

*There's only so far we can get with technological improvements*

### 3. Prioritizing email

Google is a believer that you can often use technology to solve large complex problems. So with email, the problem is the hundreds of letters that come at you; they're not all equally important. Right now, most email systems just have one huge inbox, where emails are tiered up by what time they arrived. Now, imagine that these were all physical pieces of mail. Your assistant would sort the mail, tossing the junk and separating personal letters, bills, and urgent correspondence. Now, Google has created this technology called Magic Inbox to sort your mail based on priority. My mail gets put into four piles: mail I need to look at every hour, by the end of the day, every two days, or by the end of the week.

### 4. Reviewing the week

Google has also developed a tool called Week Grinder to analyze your calendar and give you statistics on how you're spending your time. It shows how much time you spent in meetings, how much time you spent on certain projects. This is so important because your calendar never lies.

### 5. Making meetings more efficient…

We have video conferencing set up so that you can attend a meeting at your desk, instead of traveling across campus. Every meeting needs to have an agenda and a decision maker. No more than seven or eight people should be at a meeting. And meeting minutes are transcribed, so you can subscribe to the mailing list to see what is discussed in a meeting.

## 6. ...But still keeping them personal

Once a week, when I meet with my team, we share fun stories from the weekend. We also do a Power of Appreciation exercise, in which we go around the table and say something we appreciate about the person sitting next to us. Other times, we do a Gratitude practice, in which we share one thing we're grateful for. This helps to anchor us in the present moment. I also bring a bouquet of flowers and we vote on which team member should receive the flowers for that week.

These are all the tips and technologies I've come up with to optimize my work experience and make my day go smoothly so I can flourish in the "lion's den." But there's only so far we can get with technological improvements like Magic Inbox and video conferencing. So the most important way that I keep grounded and balanced is through my daily yoga and meditation practice. Through this practice, I'm able to weather any storm.

# LEARNING IN THE NEW WORLD OF WORK

In today's fast-paced, complex world, we are constantly challenged to come up with new ways to help people learn. At Adobe we do this by focusing on learning that integrates three key components: technology through on-demand learning, relationships through social learning, and self through everyday learning.

## Technology: On-demand learning

We've moved our focus for how people learn from an occasional "big gulp" to "many sips." We've all been to two- or three-day programs, at the end of which we can't really remember much—and certainly, not much changes.

Now it's possible to stay connected with others in ways that weren't possible even five years ago. We are using our virtual classroom environment technology to share information and encourage discussion, and to provide another method of communication through global team meetings and virtual meetings.

For example, this year Adobe is rolling out an evolved management curriculum. What was once a simple, two-day classroom introduction to Adobe's management philosophies and practices is now a multi-month Management Essentials Experience. New managers are placed in cohort groups and are immersed in the management experience through pre-event work (available online), through a live day-long event focused on discussion and on sharing best practices, and through applied learning assignments. Through a Management Essentials blog, the cohort groups also take discussions online by sharing real-world problems and lessons learned.

# MELISSA DAIMLER

*Melissa Daimler is currently Head of Global Learning at Adobe Systems, Inc., where she previously co-founded and led Organizational Development. She earned her M.S. in Organizational Development from Pepperdine University and has over twenty years of experience in learning and development. She is passionate about helping people use professional experiences to grow personally. Follow Melissa on Twitter @mdaimler.*

### Relationships: Social learning

At Adobe, we have a dedicated team that champions learning within the organization. It's a small team, but it works because the responsibility for successful learning is now shared by leaders across all levels of the company—from vice presidents to new college graduates.

Similar to the concept of "pay it forward," part of our learning strategy is that program participants are expected to contribute to other programs. Teaching has become an opportunity to "learn twice," and Adobe cultivates development in a continuous cycle in order to grow leaders at all levels.

Over the past year, more than a hundred leaders have volunteered to be panelists, facilitate management development programs, and lead discussions on strategy for our emerging leaders. Our leaders can spend as much as forty hours teaching and sharing best practices over a six-month period.

We have always had a leadership pipeline, and now we have a "teaching pipeline"—people who model leadership in both what they are doing and how they're leading.

### Self: Everyday learning

Learning and development at Adobe is not just about helping employees get to the next rung of the corporate ladder—although that's part of it. It is also about helping employees learn more about themselves within the organization to help them progress along their individual paths, fulfill their personal potential, and contribute to the greater good.

*Teaching has become an opportunity to "learn twice."*

We learn and practice our purpose through everyday lessons. Adobe encourages employees to "learn and grow in place" in the context of their work environment, rather than waiting for a retreat or an off-site program to help them find their bigger purpose.

For example, one of our leaders in India pulled together a team of employees to come up with an idea and develop a new product within a limited timeframe. When he created the team, he didn't select employees based on tenure, rank, or even specific skill sets—he wanted people with a passion for learning through experience and a drive to affect the business. The team succeeded in creating a product within a couple months, but the higher-level benefit was that his team was greatly energized and is now taking what they learned from this successful project and hoping to apply it to future project ideas. This is what everyday learning means at Adobe.

The world's best talent will have access to the best opportunities. The nature of these opportunities is constantly expanding to allow an ever larger group to learn through technology, each other, and purpose. Work gives us the opportunity to grow, find, and share ourselves as well as to define the work we want to do and the person we want to become. We can all be great leaders.

## THE POWER OF THE MUNDANE

Great work is often built on the mundane.

Great cathedrals start with bricks, great paintings begin with paint, and great novels start with words. No one ever castigated F. Scott Fitzgerald for failing to invent new words—his brilliance lay in how he used the exact same twenty-six letters we all use in English. No one ever complained that Picasso failed to invent new colors—his brilliance (or a major part of it, at least) was in the way he combined colors that already exist to form something new and original. And while Gaudi may have come close, even he didn't invent new shapes—he "merely" used the existing constraints of three dimensions in ways we'd never seen before.

And though it may not always seem so grand, just like Fitzgerald, Picasso, and Gaudi, as managers and leaders, every day we engage with the mundane to (hopefully) create something great. And for me, the tool I use that most helps me accelerate that process is something truly mundane: templates.

In the world of information engineers (which we all are these days), our raw materials are blocks of raw information that we need to somehow transform into something great—a plan, a proposal, a report, a blueprint, a book, a product, a speech, a presentation, a conversation... whatever it is that you do each day. And it's in how we interpret those blocks of raw data—and even more important, how we communicate our interpretation—that greatness lies.

The step where I get bogged down—and which causes me to produce merely good work, as opposed to great work—is the literal, physical act of transforming my personal insight about mundane data into

## LES MCKEOWN

*Les McKeown is the author of* Predictable Success: Getting Your Organization on the Growth Track, *and a consultant and thought leader on organizational and business growth. This Les McKeown has never played for the Bay City Rollers. Follow Les on Twitter at @lesmckeown and on the Web at* PredictableSuccess.com.

something readable by others. Whether the end result needs to be a two-by-two graph, a blog post, a book chapter, an email, a spreadsheet, a PDF, a Web-ready image, a Web page, a snip of video or audio, or an article for an insanely great compilation like this, the point at which I can lose my enthusiasm, begin to get unfocused, or just lose my way because it is so tiresome, is in translating my insight into the final "product."

That's why I have templates. Literally hundreds of them. They're all filed and tagged so I can recover them easily and instantly. I have templates for every common output model I use (see the list above), and once I envision the shape of the output I want, I can pull up the appropriate template and start producing the final product right away.

Does this mean that there's a sameness (or worse, a staleness) to everything I do? I hope not, because the time, energy, and enthusiasm I would have wasted trying to create from scratch a two-by-two graph or the structure of an email is instead invested in making this graph or this email "sing."

I've built up my template inventory over the last ten years, and I continue to add to it regularly. It saves me literally hours of work every single day, and more important, it allows me to direct my creative energies almost exclusively into making each individual piece of work I produce great (or at least as great as I can make it).

*No one ever complained that Picasso failed to invent new colors.*

## RECONSIDER YOUR APPROACH TO ORGANIZATION

Working differently starts with understanding the barriers that limit your impact. After all, work is done for a purpose. We should change the way we work only after discovering better ways to spend our enery and overcome the obstacles before us.

Here are four things to think about as you change the way you work.

### Avoid reactionary workflows

We live in a connected world of endless emails, texts, tweets, messages on social networks, phone calls, instant messages... the list goes on. Rather than be proactive with our energy, we have become reactive—living at the mercy of the last incoming thing. As a result, we spend all of our energy trying to keep up, rather than propelling our ideas forward. Eventually, all of the small inconsequential activity wears us down and we're liable to jump ship.

To avoid reactionary workflows, some people schedule "windows of non-stimulation" in their day. For a two – to three-hour period of time, they minimize their email and all other sources of incoming communication. With this time, they focus on a list of goals—not their regular tasks, but long-term items that require research and deep thought. There are other tricks for aggregating messages and reducing "hop time" (the time spent transitioning between sources of communication). But the bottom line is that a reactionary workflow is a threat to ingenuity. To combat it, we must focus less on ideas themselves and more on how we manage our energy and ultimately push ideas to completion.

## SCOTT BELSKY

*Scott Belsky believes that the greatest break-throughs across all industries are a result of creative people and teams that are especially productive. As the founder and CEO of Behance, he leads a company that develops products and services that boost productivity in the creative-professional community. Scott is also the author of the national best-selling book,* Making Ideas Happen. *Follow Scott on Twitter at @scottbelsky and on the Web at www.Behance.com.*

*The bottom line is that a reactionary workflow is a threat to ingenuity.*

## Use design-centric systems to stay organized

Every project in life can ultimately be reduced to just three primary elements: action steps, backburner items, and references.

Action steps are succinct tasks that start with verbs. They should be kept separate from your notes and sketches.

Backburner items are ideas that come up during a brainstorm or on the run that are not actionable now but might be someday. Backburner items should be collected in a central location and should be revisited periodically through some sort of ritual.

The third element of every project is references—the articles, notes, and other stuff that collects around you. It turns out that references are overrated. Rather than spend tons of time organizing your notes, consider keeping a file where all your notes are simply filed chronologically (not by project name or other means). In the age of digital calendars, you can search for any meeting and quickly find the notes taken on that date.

The color, texture, size, and style of the materials used to capture your tasks (and your notes) are important. People who have successfully developed personal systems for productivity over the years claim that their designs make their projects more appealing (and thus more likely to be managed well). When it comes to productivity, attraction breeds loyalty.

## Measure meetings with action steps

Meetings are extremely expensive if you consider the cost of time and interruptions. Beware of "Posting Meetings" or meeting just because it's Monday. Such meetings are often planned for the morning—when you're most productive—and often end without any action steps captured. A meeting that ends without any action steps should have been a voicemail or an email.

When you do meet with clients or colleagues, end each meeting with a quick review of captured action steps. The exercise takes less than 30 seconds per person. Each person should share what he captured. Doing so will almost always reveal a few action steps that were either missed, duplicated, or misunderstood. Stating your action steps aloud also breeds a sense of accountability.

## Reduce Insecurity Work

In the era of Google Analytics and Twitter, we spend too much time obsessing over real-time data. Just a decade ago, we had to wait for weekly and monthly reports to get information that is now always available at our fingertips. Whether you are checking your site's traffic, customer sentiment, or your bank account, these small repetitive actions don't help you make ideas happen. They just help you feel safe.

"Insecurity Work" is stuff you do that (1) has no intended outcome, (2) does not move the ball forward in any way, and (3) is quick enough that you can do it multiple times a day without realizing it—but nonetheless puts you at ease. The first step in reducing Insecurity Work is gaining self-awareness. The ways and means of reducing this distraction are nearly infinite—I've been astonished by the spectrum of self-imposed guidelines and very effective rituals that people use to reduce Insecurity Work.

Before you change the way you work, be introspective. Consider why you do what you do. Start to make small changes. Measure your progress. Then do it again.

# GET PHYSICAL

*"The ideal attitude is to be physically loose
and mentally tight."*

Arthur Ashe,
Champion tennis player

There's a dilemma in the world of running. Even as the technology in our running shoes gets ever fancier—new gels, springs, materials, and padding—running injuries keep on recurring: bad knees, bad ankles, shin splints.

In some part of the running community, a new movement is growing in response to these chronic injuries—barefoot running. Running without shoes uses quite different mechanics from running with shoes and creates a different form of connection with the world around you.

None of these contributors are proponents of barefoot running. But they are champions for reconnecting with our physical bodies as a source of wisdom, balance, and productivity. Too many of us consider our bodies simply as devices for carrying around our brains. These contributors suggest otherwise.

## IN THIS SECTION

## UNPLUG

In brief: What's the message here? The message is, we get one life. We should spend less of that one life hunched over a device.

It was closing in on midnight. I heard the sound of chairs scraping on the floor overhead. Then I heard my housemates yelling. What happened in the next twelve hours was life changing. The house I shared with five housemates burned to the ground.

Bearing witness to your house burning down is not what most of us would choose as an opportunity to return to the present moment. Yet there's tenderness in catastrophe. Here's what catastrophe does. It asks you to evaluate your life in an instant: what matters?

What matters? The fire marshal asks it differently. He walks into your neighbor's house, where you've set up camp. He wipes soot off his face with the back of his hand. Then he asks, "In the unlikely event you're permitted to go back in there, what are you going to grab? Make a list."

You realize something when you don't know what's left of what you own. You're fully equipped with all that you need now, in the present moment. This very body. This very breath. You've got that. In a simple, refreshing way, when you're taking stock of what's left after catastrophe, what you really sense is how alive your body is. How each breath breathes you. In deep sadness and loss, you witness delight. You're alive.

In nearly ten years of living life online, more than seven of them blogging and the past four on the social Web, I've made these observations about the body's response to digital life. Technology tends to numb

## GWEN BELL

*Gwen Bell is a social Web strategist. She is also a yoga practitioner. Her work, including her eBook,* Digital Warriorship, *explores how these worlds meet. Follow Gwen on Twitter at @gwenbell and on the Web at GwenBell.com.*

*Honestly evaluate how much of your life you're spending consuming information. Consider how much of your life you'd spend on that if you knew tonight that your house would catch fire.*

us. We sit at our computers, diaphragms closed off, decreasing our lung capacity. When we're not hunched over our computers, we're bent sideways over devices, shortening the muscles in our backs.

For technologists and knowledge workers, building wellness into the day shouldn't be optional. My mission is to change the wellness of knowledge workers from perceived luxury to understood necessity.

If you're reading this, you're a consumer of information. According to research from the University of California, San Diego, we consume nearly three times as much information today than was consumed in 1960. We're consuming this information in the morning before we roll out of bed. We're consuming it on the toilet. The last thing we do before we fall asleep? Consume information.

## What we consume, consumes us.

The antidote to this lack of awareness is, simply, practicing awareness. Bringing our minds into the present frees us. Here's how to get started with that:

### 1. Think about your Information Consumption Posture

How do you stand when you're on the phone? How do you sit while working on your laptop at a café? Cultivate mindfulness about your body. Keep a log and record self-observations about your posture, energy, and effectiveness throughout the day. Becoming present to yourself is the first step. Bear witness to your own life.

### 2. Eliminate one thing from your workflow

Can you check email less frequently during your day? Can you take a social networking app off your phone? What's no longer serving you as a technologist? What's a distraction? And when you've removed one, eliminate a second.

### 3. Add something positive to your workflow

Practice sitting in the morning. Watch your breath come and go for ten minutes to start. Add applications to your computer that remind you to take breaks (Time Out), ask you your intention before you log in (GMail Extensions), and track your time online (Rescue Time).

Ask for support as you take this plunge into yourself and out of the life-affirming (but time-wasting) practice of what Scott Belsky calls Insecurity Work. You don't have to get an alert each time someone mentions your name on the Web. You don't have to respond emotionally each time your company gets an online hit.

Honestly evaluate how much of your life you're spending consuming information. Consider how much of your life you'd spend on that if you knew tonight that your house would catch fire. We shouldn't need our lives to catch fire to live like our lives mean something. With or without the Web, we exist.

With or without the Internet, our bodies need movement and tenderness. We can't think our way to that tender place; we have to move ourselves into it.

## CREDIBILITY IS THE FOUNDATION OF LEADERSHIP

Leadership begins with you and your belief in yourself. Leadership continues only if other people also believe in you.

All the programs to develop leaders, all the courses and classes, all the books and tapes, all the blogs and websites offering tips and techniques, are meaningless unless the people who are supposed to follow believe in the person who's supposed to lead.

The truth is that credibility is the foundation of leadership. This is the inescapable conclusion we've come to after thirty years of asking thousands of people around the world what they look for and admire in a leader, someone whose direction they would willingly follow. The key word in the preceding sentence is "willingly." It's one thing to follow someone because you think you have to, "or else," and it's another when you follow a leader because you want to. What does it take to be the kind of leader others want to follow?

It turns out that the believability of the leader trumps everything else. Leader credibility determines whether people will willingly give more of their time, talent, energy, experience, intelligence, creativity, and support. It's also the strongest influencer of unit profitability and performance. Only credible leaders earn commitment, and only commitment builds and regenerates great organizations and communities.

The data have been so strong and so consistent for so long that we've come to refer to this principle as The Kouzes-Posner First Law of Leadership: If you don't believe in the messenger, you won't believe the message.

## JIM KOUZES AND BARRY POSNER

*Jim Kouzes and Barry Posner have co-authored over thirty books and workbooks on leadership and leadership development, including the award-winning* The Leadership Challenge. *Jim is a professional speaker and the Dean's Executive Fellow of Leadership, Leavey School of Business, Santa Clara University, and Barry is Professor of Leadership and former Dean at the Leavey School of Business, Santa Clara University. Follow Jim and Barry on the Web at LeadershipChallenge.com.*

*Strengthening your credibility comes down to one thing. You have to go first as a leader. You have to be the example that others can follow.*

### Seeing is believing

The data confirm that credibility is the foundation of leadership. But what is credibility behaviorally? How do you know it when you see it?

The answer we hear is always the same. It's some version of "Do what you say you will do," or DWYSYWD for short. There are lots of other common phrases for it. "Walk the talk," "practice what you preach," "put your money where your mouth is," "keep your promise," and "follow through on your commitments" are a few. They all mean the same thing. Your actions had better be consistent with your words.

"Actions speak louder than words" is wise counsel to live by. When people see you doing what you say, they have the evidence that you mean it. Otherwise it's just words. Your actions send the loudest signals about your commitment to anything. The truth is that either you lead by example or you don't lead at all.

Quite often the greatest distance leaders have to travel is the distance from their mouths to their feet. Taking that step toward fulfilling a promise, putting the resources behind a pledge, and acting on a verbal commitment may require great courage. But it's the very thing that demonstrates the courage of your convictions.

### The one question you must ask yourself every day

To earn and sustain your credibility, you must ask yourself just one question at the beginning of every day and at the end of every day. In the morning, ask: What am I going to do today to make sure that other people see my commitment to the values and beliefs, vision and mission, projects and initiatives of this organization? How will my calendar show it? How will the people I meet with show it? How will my agendas show it? How will the stories I tell show it? How will my rewards and recognitions show it? How will my hires and promotions show it?

At the end of the day, ask yourself: What did I do today to demonstrate my commitment to the values and beliefs, mission and vision, projects and initiatives of this organization? What's the evidence that I did what I said I would do?

Strengthening your credibility comes down to one thing. You have to go first as a leader. You have to be the example that others can follow.

## HOW CAN WE "DO MORE, FEEL BETTER, LIVE LONGER"?

The mission of GSK is "do more, feel better, live longer"—and our work is to help our employees internalize this mission.

We are passionate about what we do for our patients—it is a major motivating force that keeps us going when the work gets tough and the hours are long. And everything is changing—the external world is rightly demanding healthcare for all, healthcare that is a good value and accessible and safe and effective. So to deliver all this, we need to change, and we as an organization are demanding huge changes of ourselves. This means each person has to change.

Our role is to help people make choices that change how they see things, how they understand things, how they do things, and how they relate to people—to each other and most of all to themselves.

We have seen that for change to be effective, a number of things must be present:

- A consistent, understandable story about the overarching reason for change—and this must be bigger than the organization. For us, it is about getting medicines and other healthcare to our patients and customers. Our environment has changed, so we must, too.
- A clear strategy for getting to where we are going, and the ability to make it simple, logical, and easily explainable. We have five very clear strategies, and everything we do can be linked to them.
- A set of tools to help deliver the "plumbing" or the "hard-wired" changes needed—such as process simplification, a consistent change framework, project management, etc.

## SALLY BONNEYWELL, KIM LAFFERTY, AND SUE CRUSE

*Sally Bonneywell is Head of Coaching, Kim Lafferty is Head of Leadership, and Sue Cruse is Head of Health, Sustainability, and Performance at GlaxoSmithKline.*

> *We have found that human factors absolutely make the difference between fast-moving and exciting change and being overwhelmed.*

- Attention paid to the "human factors." This is for us the most critical and the most intangible ingredient of successful change.

The human factors in change are vast and complex. We have found that they absolutely make the difference between fast-moving, smooth, exciting, and fun change and the feelings of dislocation, loss, and being overwhelmed.

There are a number of interventions that, when put together, become a rich tapestry of support and reinforcement for people during these changing times.

### Coaching

Coaching is about helping people to become conscious of the choices they make. It helps develop their muscle of self-reliance—crucial when each situation is potentially a new one that demands new and original thinking from our leaders. Coaching does bring about individual transformation—helping people to "become the change" they want to see. Coaches work with leaders to help them see the meaning in their lives, to reconnect with who they really are, and to rediscover what matters most to them and how their identity, values, and behaviors align to deliver purpose in their lives. This experience brings about tremendous positive, hopeful, powerful change. By encouraging people to be curious and be present, we find that extraordinary things can happen.

### Inspirational leadership

Leaders need to be inspirational to bring others with them during challenging and turbulent times. The Inspirational Leadership

Programme at GSK brings together elements of psychology, philosophy, and the performing arts to help leaders make sense of their work in relation to their deepest values and then articulate a clear message in a compelling way. It is about looking at how different elements of your life have come together and are coalescing around key messages, actions, and ways of being that make meaning in your life and your work. People change the way they view themselves and their relationships with others—in ways that are lasting and profound—and talk to their teams about it.

## Energy and resilience

Managing energy—not just time—is the key to delivering extraordinary results. The aim is to help people consciously manage their energy so that they can be physically energized, emotionally connected, emotionally focused, and spiritually aligned. We hold Energy for Performance seminars, which help leaders become conscious of their energy and how they use it, generate it, and share it. The results have been phenomenal—people perform better at work and are more satisfied with their lives overall.

## Bringing it all together

Telling stories is an integral part of bringing all this together so that people can make sense of it—they can see how they are absolutely at the heart of any change. Making sense of change, making it sustainable, and making it happen now are part of an ongoing journey, and a fun one, too.

## REWARDS, THREATS, AND WHAT TRULY MOTIVATES PEOPLE

There are just a few core factors that drive human social behavior. Your brain is keeping track of each of these domains at all times—in fact, every 0.2 seconds. It's looking for opportunities to get more of them, and to an even greater extent it's looking for ways to avoid having them be reduced.

These factors are not, as popular wisdom often has it, based on money or extrinsic rewards. Neuroscience has helped us discover what really motivates people. The SCARF acronym is a simple way of remembering what these factors are: Status, Certainty, Autonomy, Relatedness, Fairness.

When you get any of the SCARF drivers, the reward circuitry in your brain is activated. But if any of them are reduced, the threat circuitry in your brain is triggered.

Now, the important thing to understand is that negative input is much more influential than positive input. Your brain puts more emphasis on minimizing danger than it does on maximizing reward.

Studies show that if you tell someone "You look great today," he'll forget about the compliment soon after. But if you tell him something negative—that he looks like a mess today—that insult will reverberate over and over and over. When you put someone in a scanner and show him an angry face and a happy face, the brain lights up much more for the angry face.

This concept is crucial to understand because this fundamental towards/away-from dynamic is at the heart of a lot of the

## DR. DAVID ROCK

*Dr. David Rock has led the field of neuro-leadership, connecting the latest discoveries of how our brains work with what it means to manage and lead. He is the CEO of Results Coaching Systems and the author of several books, including* Your Brain at Work *and* Coaching With Your Brain in Mind. *Follow David on Twitter at @davidrock101 and on the Web at DavidRock.net, and see him speak as part of the TEDx series.*

misunderstandings, reactions, arguments, and threats that occur that inhibit good neural functioning. And that has a direct influence on how people—and therefore teams and therefore organizations—function effectively, and in the end, succeed or don't succeed.

## Using SCARF to manage and motivate

So how do these learnings translate into tactics for managing your team?

First, it's important to realize that money isn't intrinsically motivating in many situations. If you give someone a bonus, but the circumstances are unfair, she might feel angry and threatened rather than rewarded. And when you recognize that autonomy is a reward in most situations, you'll let your staff have more responsibility and make more choices—and this will be more rewarding than a bonus.

What we've learned about status is that people are much more comfortable when the hierarchy is clear. We're always trying to figure out who's dominant in a given situation, and we feel better once we know. If your status is threatened, the response is visceral. So we've found that it's helpful to have a clear hierarchy in an organization, but it's very counterproductive to unintentionally create status threats.

The best way to mitigate the strength of negative inputs is to create opportunities for reward. Instead of telling a team member what she did wrong, ask her what she would do differently next time. This gives the person a chance to shine.

*Your brain puts more emphasis on minimizing danger than it does on maximizing reward.*

## THE 15-MINUTE SECRET

Almost all of you, I'm willing to bet, have a "morning ritual."

But how many of you have created one by design? This is so important to individual effectiveness, for everyone but especially for entrepreneurs who work independently or at home.

I first became aware of the idea when interviewing a pair of salesmen for my first book. Together, they did an early-morning gym session followed by a brainstorm, a process they called "day-righting." After about a month of this routine, they saw dramatic improvements in their business and their lives.

So, what's your version of day-righting? I travel so much and keep such an erratic schedule that my day-righting isn't so much a morning process as a daily commitment to an hour-long workout, usually a social one, wherever I am.

But for those of you who start every morning at a fairly reliable time, I guarantee that designing a morning ritual will help you be more relaxed, more focused, and more productive throughout the day.

Here are some ideas to play with:

Exercise: You may not be a "morning exerciser" or have time for a full session, but even ten minutes of movement (a high-intensity run or a yoga session) can prepare you for solid thinking.

Journaling: Spend five minutes reflecting, in writing, on the past day or night, and five minutes jotting down your expectations for today.

## KEITH FERRAZZI

*Keith Ferrazzi is the world's foremost expert in professional relationship development. At the heart of his work is this insight: Generosity in relationships is the cornerstone of success. He's the author of* Never Eat Alone *and* Who's Got Your Back. *Follow Keith on Twitter at @keithferrazzi and on the Web at KeithFerrazzi.com.*

Meditation: Meditation is a powerful routine—but many of us struggle to make it a distinct daily activity. You can "hack" this by blending meditation into your existing routines, such as by doing a walking meditation.

Breathing: Breathe in deeply. Hold it in. Exhale. Hold it out. Repeat ten times. This in itself is a form of meditation.

*So, what's your version of day-righting?*

## LIVING THE BRAND

I remember walking around the streets of Hollis, Queens, as a little boy and feeling a new sort of energy in the community. Many people will tell you that energy came from the emergence of this new music genre called hip-hop, but it goes much further than that. You see, when Hollis natives like Russell Simmons, the members of Salt-N-Pepa (Cheryl James, Sandy Denton, and Deidra "Dee Dee" Roper), and LL Cool J became superstars, their fans didn't idolize them for only their music. There was an obsession among millions of people, including myself, who admired how these rappers walked, talked, and most important, dressed.

That energy was less about a new type of music and more about the birth of a new lifestyle.

After FUBU turned into a multibillion-dollar brand, many other companies tried to emulate our formula, but failed. Their mistakes had to do with the assumption that FUBU succeeded solely because it appealed to a new demographic. Thinking that this was the way to communicate to African-Americans, companies began putting rapping, bald black guys in their ads. You can still see this problem today with the rise of Latin-targeted advertisements. When they put a white guy speaking Spanish in a commercial, that doesn't mean that it will attract the Latin community.

Remember, the easiest thing to sell is the truth.

Consumers could see that the messaging of these new brands wasn't authentic, so they didn't buy it. These companies didn't understand that what drove FUBU, as well as the handful of other similar fashion lines, to success was that its creators were living the brand and were

## DAYMOND JOHN

*Daymond John is CEO and founder of FUBU, a much-celebrated global lifestyle brand and a pioneer in the fashion industry, with over $6 billion in product sales. He is an award-winning entrepreneur, and he has received more than thirty-five awards, including Brandweek Marketer of the Year, the Advertising Age Marketing 1000 Award for Outstanding Ad Campaign, and Ernst & Young's New York Entrepreneur of the Year Award.*

*Remember, the easiest thing*
*to sell is the truth.*

able to communicate this effectively. Once people started to catch on, they embraced the brands that were truly made for us and by us.

The key that many companies and brands miss is that simply being different is not enough. By focusing their energy on figuring out how they can stand out from their competitors, they suddenly become passive, reactionary companies, and they dismiss the most important element of their business—living the brand they market. Unless you partner with someone or hire a professional spokesperson who specializes in what you're marketing, you're left with no choice but to fully understand the brand by living it. You will find that when you practice what you preach, you're already about your brand, and that will simplify the way you communicate about it.

Consumers know when you're not being authentic, and when this occurs, your brand will instantly be tainted.

The big idea here is that you can't just be about it; you need to live it.

You have no idea how often the power of authenticity is overlooked. Even when I'm consulting with top brands, it always goes back to making sure the message is delivered in the appropriate tone, language, and communication channels. If you don't, how else will consumers understand you and your brand?

## THE 90-MINUTE PLAN

For nearly a decade now, I've begun my workdays by focusing for 90 minutes, uninterrupted, on the task I decide the night before is the most important one I'll face the following day. After 90 minutes, I take a break.

To make this possible, I turn off my email while I'm working, close all windows on my computer, and let the phone go to voicemail if it rings.

I typically get more work done during those 90 minutes, and feel more satisfied with my output, than I do for any comparable period of time the rest of the day. It can be tough on some days to fully focus for 90 minutes, but I always have a clear stopping time, which makes it easier.

I launched this practice because I discovered that my energy, my will, and my capacity for intense focus diminish as the day wears on. Anything really challenging that I put off tends not to get done, and it's the most difficult work that tends to generate the greatest enduring value.

I first made this discovery while writing a book—and wanting to break some old patterns.

I'd previously written three books, and for each one, I'd dutifully sit down at my desk at 7 a.m., and I'd often stay there until 7 p.m. During that time, I probably spent more time avoiding writing than I did actually writing. Instead, I spent an inordinate amount of time and energy on making lists, responding to email, answering the phone, and keeping my desk clean and my files incredibly well organized.

## TONY SCHWARTZ

*Tony Schwartz's most recent book,* How To Be Excellent at Anything, *tackles the challenge of how we can best find, conserve, and focus our energy, our most precious resource. He is the CEO of The Energy Project. Follow Tony on Twitter at @tonyschwartz and on the Web at TheEnergyProject.com.*

*Finding an excuse to avoid hard work isn't hard to do.*

There were days I never got to writing at all. It was incredibly frustrating.

To make the change, I decided to build highly precise, deliberate practices, done at specific times, so they would eventually become automatic and wouldn't require much expenditure of energy or self-discipline. They would be akin to brushing my teeth at night.

The effect of these practices on my efficiency was staggering. I wrote my fourth book in less than half the time I had invested in any of the three previous ones.

Here are the three key steps to building this habit.

## Choose

I choose the next day's work the night before because I don't want to squander energy thinking about what to do during the time I've set aside to actually do the work.

I define "important" as whatever it is I believe will add the most enduring value if I get it done. More often than not, that means a challenge that is "important but not urgent," to use Steven Covey's language. These are precisely the activities we most often put off—in favor of those that are more urgent, are easier to accomplish, and provide more immediate gratification.

## Start

I start at a very specific time because I discovered early on that when I didn't hold myself to an exact time, it became a license to procrastinate. "Oh wait," I'd tell myself, "I'm just going to answer this email."

Before I knew it, I'd have answered a dozen emails, and a half-dozen more had arrived, calling out for my attention.

Finding an excuse to avoid hard work isn't hard to do.

## Stop

I work for 90 minutes because that's what the research suggests is the optimal human limit for focusing intensely on any given task. Researcher Peretz Lavie calls this our "ultradian rhythm" and it governs our energy levels.

Over the course of 90 minutes, especially when we're maximally focused, we move from a relatively high state of energy down into a physiological trough.

Many of us unwittingly train ourselves to ignore our bodies' signals that we need a rest—difficulty concentrating, physical restlessness, irritability. Instead, we find ways to override this need with caffeine, sugar, and our own stress hormones—adrenalin, noradrenalin, and cortisol—all of which provide short bursts of energy but leave us over-aroused.

By intentionally aligning with my body's natural rhythms, I've learned to listen to its signals. When I notice them, it usually means I've hit the 90-minute mark. At that point, I take a break, even if I feel I'm on a roll, because I've learned that if I don't, I'll pay the price later in the day.

Choose. Start. Stop. I don't get it right every day, but this single 90-minute practice has been life changing for me.

# COLLABORATE

*"In the long history of humankind (and animal kind, too) those who learned to collaborate and improvise most effectively have prevailed."*

Charles Darwin,
Scientist

I love tiramisu. Blame it on my first girlfriend and her Italian family. Or maybe on the clever name, translated as "pick me up."

Take a look at the ingredients. A few of them I like a lot—coffee and liquor in particular. Other ingredients, I'm generally indifferent to—Ladyfinger biscuits, mascarpone, egg yolks, and cocoa.

But put them together and let them sit for a while, and magic happens.

This isn't a cooking section, but it is a place where the contributors encourage you to find your own ingredients and create a recipe for success.

## IN THIS SECTION

## RIDING WITH THE POSSE

You're feeling tired and frazzled—overcome with deadlines and emails. Perhaps now is the time to learn how to assemble and ride with a posse.

I first learnt this term when I asked Inez, a rookie management consultant, how she got her job done. She pointed to her computer screen, along the bottom of which was arrayed a row of names and faces, and she told me: "This is my posse. They ride with me and we help each other out."

Your posse is a small group of people—five, ten, rarely more than fifteen—whom you can call on and trust to help you when the going gets tough. Your friendship with them might go back years or just weeks. Some will work in the same place as you, others not. Some you'll see all the time, while others could be in a different country.

My experience with Inez and her posse reminded me of the story of Frank and Fred that I've told elsewhere. It goes something like this:

Both were given a really tough project to complete at breakneck speed.

Fred knew immediately what to do: he had to close down and concentrate. First, he rang his wife to say he would be home late for the next couple of weeks—he knew this was a job that would totally consume him. Then he closed his office door and told his PA not to disturb him. He began to figure out what he needed to do and to draw up the project plans. Fred's view of his work was that this was a big task that only he could solve. Of course, he acknowledged that he would have to bring in other skills at times to work on the details, but it was he who was the master planner. Only he could really tackle the challenge, and with this in mind he wanted to remain undisturbed in order to truly focus.

## LYNDA GRATTON

*Lynda Gratton is Professor of Management Practice at London Business School and the founder of the Hot Spot Movement. She's the author of several books, including* Glow: How You Can Radiate Energy, Innovation and Success *and* The Shift: Why the Future of Work Is Here Now. *Follow Lynda on Twitter at @lyndagratton and on the Web at HotSpotsMovement.com.*

*Now is the time to learn how to assemble and ride with a posse.*

Frank took the opposite approach. The first thing he did was to remember the people he knew who might help him, and within minutes he had phoned a couple of them to ask their opinions. One person was a dear friend whom he had worked with over ten years ago, and who he knew had faced a similar challenge. In five minutes, she'd provided Frank with some critical advice about three factors that could derail the project. Next, Frank called someone he had met more recently and whom he had helped out only last week. This person had in-depth knowledge of some of the technical aspects of the project and gave Frank his point of view on how to structure the approach. In the time Fred had closed his door and spoken to his PA, Frank had already begun to assemble his posse.

So do you tend to be a Fred? Or are you more of a Frank?

Here are three insights on how to best assemble your own posse:

1.  Assemble a relatively small group of people who have some of the same expertise in common—with sufficient overlap to really understand each other and add value quickly. This overlap is crucial to speed.

2.  Build relationships of trust, generosity, and mutual support. The posse members trust you—they have ridden out with you before. These are folks you have known for some time and who like and support you.

3.  Hone your cooperative skills. Become skilled at mentoring, learn how to make the best of diversity, and work on your ability to communicate with people, especially if they are in another location.

The posse will come to your aid because they are on your side, can understand what you are up against, and can help you quickly and without distracting you. They are going to be crucial to how you work more smoothly—and how you stay more Frank than Fred.

## REFLECTIONS

What do you value most?

Does your work reflect that?

These are the gut-check questions I ask myself when I am frustrated with bad work or bored with merely good work. Align what you do with what you value, and fantastic things happen.

I'm a tech writer or a software developer, depending on what minute of the day you catch me. There are three values I hold dear: service, collaboration, and publicness.

### Service

Great work is doing stuff that gives back to the world, as well as serving your own purposes. It's the difference between writing things down to remember them versus writing things down to teach others. For me, writing about technology does both. But having knowledge isn't nearly as meaningful as sharing it. For me, great work is about service.

### Collaboration

Wisdom is knowing what you don't know. Assuming that others know more than you do opens you up to collaborative relationships that can push you to unexpected heights. My favorite fable in the world, "Stone Soup," is a metaphor for building open-source software and realizing the power of collaboration. I try to simmer a fresh bowl whenever possible. For me, great work is about collaboration.

## GINA TRAPANI

*Gina Trapani is a project director at Expert Labs, a nonprofit organization that helps policy makers in the U.S. government take advantage of the expertise of their fellow citizens. Her project, ThinkUp, is an open-source social-media-insights platform, which is available to download for free. Gina was the first editor of Lifehacker.com. Follow Gina on Twitter at @ginatrapani and on the Web at ThinkUpApp.com and GinaTrapani.org.*

*Align what you do with what you value, and fantastic things happen.*

## Publicness

Service and collaboration require some degree of publicness, and with public great work comes recognition and reputation. That, in turn, creates bigger and better opportunities for collaboration and service. When you're recognized for great work, more people want to work with you and help you help others—it's a virtuous cycle. For me, publicness is inherent in growing great work.

Last year I had the opportunity to turn a weekend software project into a tool that the White House uses to more efficiently gather feedback from U.S. citizens. It's the highest purpose I could have imagined for a spare-time project that I'd built for my own use, and the opportunity arose only because of this process of alignment.

What do you value most?

Does your work reflect that?

# MUPPET MARKETING

South Africa has over 5 million people living with HIV/AIDS. An estimated 330,000 of them are under the age of 14. The impact of the virus extends well beyond this group; there are nearly 2 million "AIDS orphans"—children (under age 19) whose parents died from AIDS, accounting for more than half the orphans in the nation.

These are problems no child should be faced with.

For decades, Sesame Workshop has been leveraging the power of media to improve the lives of children around the world. Tackling HIV/AIDS awareness among young children is something South Africa needed assistance with, and we were able to help. But we could not get there alone. We partnered with the local broadcaster, the South African Broadcast Company ("SABC"), the United States Agency for International Development (USAID), and Sanlam Life to create Takalani Sesame, a localized co-production of Sesame Street. In addition to our typical focus on literacy and numeracy, Takalani Sesame has a special focus on HIV/AIDS awareness and safety. The show aims to reduce the stigma around the disease and to promote tolerance of those who have it.

Together, we developed Kami, a new Muppet who is HIV-positive. She was designed with the HIV/AIDS epidemic in mind. A disproportionate number of girls and women in South Africa are HIV-positive, so Kami is female. Kami is asymptomatic to counter misconceptions that HIV-positive people are sickly. And because of the large number of AIDS orphans in the country, Kami is one as well—her mother died of an AIDS-related illness. Kami was adopted by a human family on Takalani Sesame in order to model positive community and family interaction.

## GARY KNELL

*Gary Knell is President and Chief Executive Officer of Sesame Workshop. Mr. Knell leads the nonprofit educational organization in its mission to create innovative, engaging content that maximizes the educational power of all media to help children reach their highest potential. He has been instrumental in focusing the organization on Sesame Street's global mission, including groundbreaking co-productions in South Africa, India, Northern Ireland, and Egypt. He also helped found PBS Kids Sprout, a 24-hour domestic cable channel in the U.S. Mr. Knell holds a BA in Political Science and Journalism from the University of California at Los Angeles and a JD from Loyola University School of Law.*

*Getting there was a team effort. These problems are too big to successfully tackle alone.*

Together, Sesame Workshop and our partners brought Kami to the children—and caregivers—of South Africa. We have produced more than 400 television episodes of Takalani Sesame. Through our partners and funders, we have distributed more than a million pieces of print materials—necessary tools, given the eleven official languages in South Africa. And through our Takalani Sesame "Talk to Me" campaign, aimed at caregivers, we have distributed half a million educational kits and developed hundreds of radio episodes.

The effect: dramatic. With an annual investment of roughly $6 million, we've been able to reach roughly 6 million South African children, both urban and rural—that's $1 per year, per child. Among these children, we've seen measurable gains in literacy, math, and HIV/AIDS knowledge and tolerance. The gains also apply to caregivers—those exposed to the Talk to Me campaign were two times more likely to talk to their children about HIV.

Each day, Takalani Sesame helps improve the lives of children. Getting there was a team effort. These problems are too big to successfully tackle alone.

# THE IMPORTANCE OF FAILURE

All too often, leaders do everything they can to avoid failure. That makes sense in a world where success is defined by operational excellence. But today, business has its roots in innovation and risk taking, where failure is a natural outcome. And especially in a service-driven business, failure is an everyday occurrence.

I'm not asking that you just accept failure; instead, I'm asking that you make your organization resilient in the face of failure so that you can confidently and more aggressively embrace risk. Otherwise, you and your organization will take on only those new risks that have a high chance of success, because the perceived penalties of failure are too high. And these changes will be so incremental that the impact on your bottom line will be incremental as well.

There are a few things you can do to improve the resilience of your organization.

## Celebrate risk taking and failure

How many times have you encouraged your team to take risks? That's not enough—you also have to highlight when someone has decided to take a risk, as that's the most precarious time for him, when he needs the support. In the same vein, you also have to celebrate the outcome, and celebrate with equal gusto whether the project is a failure or a success. Otherwise, your innovators will focus on risk mitigation rather than focusing on what is needed to make the initiative a roaring success.

## CHARLENE LI

*Charlene Li is the Founder of Altimeter Group and the author of* Open Leadership: How Social Technology Can Transform the Way You Lead. *You can follow Charlene on Twitter at @charleneli and on the Web at altimetergroup.com.*

*I'm not asking that you just accept failure; instead, make your organization resilient in the face of failure.*

### Reward people who bring forward failures

Nobody wants to be the bearer of bad news, but if you as a manager don't know what is going wrong, how can you be expected to help fix it? Stephen Elop, the current CEO of Nokia, explained to me that he encourages people to come to him early with problems so that he can apply the full brainpower and resources of the organization to help fix the problems. So he makes it a priority to make it easy for people to approach management with bad news, frequently highlighting and rewarding employees for bringing forward failures.

### Define the limits

To make transparency and risk taking more palatable to risk-averse executives, create what I call "sandbox covenants." Figure out which risks and failures are acceptable. Clearly define the walls of this sandbox and communicate the rules of engagement within those walls. Also explain what the consequences are—both to individuals and to the company—if people step outside of the sandbox. When people agree to these covenants in advance, there is greater confidence and security in knowing that the risks—and the failures—will be accepted.

## MAKING VIRTUAL TEAMS WORK

When I speak to audiences about teamwork, one of the most frequently asked—and least sexy—questions I get has to do with managing groups of people who are geographically dispersed, a.k.a. virtual teams. With so many teams these days composed of members living in different time zones and countries and on different continents, and with travel budgets likely to shrink for the foreseeable future, there probably has never been a greater need for people who don't see each other very often to figure out how to work better together. The key is simply to avoid three mistakes.

### 1. Don't underestimate the challenges of being dispersed

Because email and voicemail and texting and instant messaging have become so second-nature, we too often assume that a team member's physical location makes little difference in the effectiveness of the team. This, of course, makes no sense.

After all, no family would say, "Well, Dad lives in New York, Mom lives in San Francisco, and the kids are spread around the country, but thanks to my iPhone and computer, it's no different than living under the same roof." The simple but often overlooked truth is that without the daily interaction of breakfast or dinner or homework or late-night conversations or doing the dishes, a family can't possibly develop and maintain the strength that it needs to thrive during good times and survive during challenging ones. The same is true for teams who have no incidental conversations in the hallway or at lunch or in the elevator.

## PATRICK LENCIONI

*Patrick Lencioni is the founder and president of The Table Group, a firm dedicated to providing organizations with ideas, products, and services that improve teamwork, clarity, and employee engagement. Patrick is the author of nine best-selling books with nearly 3 million copies sold. After nine years in print, his book* The Five Dysfunctions of a Team *continues to be a fixture on national best-seller lists. Follow Patrick on the Web at TableGroup.com.*

Once a team understands the disadvantage of not being co-located, it will be more likely to take on the next mistake that virtual teams make.

## 2. Do use well the precious time you spend together

Too many virtual teams spend their quarterly or monthly in-person sessions engaging in social activities, somehow believing that this is how the team will bond. Social time is okay, but if there is not a focused and organized attempt to build relationships in the context of the work that needs to be done, then the team will only improve its collective golf scores or, worse yet, its tolerance for alcohol. On the other side of the equation, too many teams go the other way, spending their sparse time together doing detailed operations reviews and addressing overly tactical matters, and this is almost as unproductive as golfing.

The perfect storm occurs when teams split their time between irrelevant socializing and wasting time in the weeds, resulting almost inevitably in everyone's coming to dread another useless trip to corporate headquarters.

What team members really need to do when they are face-to-face is develop their relationships by getting to know one another's strengths and weaknesses, not in a touchy-feely way but in the context of the goals of the business. They need to establish clear alignment around the bigger-picture issues, like the team's core purpose, values, strategic anchors, and top priorities. Strong relationships are critical to getting on the same page because they allow the team to debate issues passionately and productively, thereby increasing the likelihood that everyone will buy in.

*No family would say, "Well, Dad lives in New York, Mom lives in San Francisco, and the kids are spread around the country, but thanks to my iPhone and computer, it's no different than living under the same roof."*

Buy-in is especially important for virtual team members because when they get back to their offices, they will need to work with a high degree of confidence that their peers will do what they agreed to do for the good of the team. That is hard enough when those peers sit in the cube or office across the hall and have plenty of in-person meetings on a regular basis. When they're in different cities, it is much more difficult—which brings us to mistake number three.

## 3. Do master the conference call

The final mistake that virtual teams make is failing to master one of the most loathed and underestimated of all corporate activities: the dreaded conference call. Even in this age of improved video-conferencing, there is simply no good, reliable, and affordable everyday substitute for the speaker phone when it comes to working with remote colleagues.

Unfortunately, just as we've done with regular meetings, we've come to believe that conference calls are inherently boring and unchangeable, a sort of corporate penance. So we accept agenda items that are neither compelling nor critical, and we make an unspoken deal with each other: "You let me check my email and play Spider Solitaire and do busywork—all with the Mute button on—and I'll keep coming to these meetings and offering my perfunctory input to let everyone know I'm still awake."

What teams have to do is make a serious commitment to one another that they will maintain a high standard of behavior during conference calls, even higher than they would for an in-person meeting. That will mean eliminating outside interruptions, avoiding distractions, foregoing the use of the Mute button, and indicating agreement or disagreement verbally to avoid passive approvals born out of misinterpreted silence.

This process all starts with the building of strong relationships, and the only way our teams are going to be willing to dedicate the time and energy to do that is if we first fully understand the disadvantage of being virtual. From that place of clarity, virtual teams can flourish.

## MAKE A DIFFERENCE WITH DESIGN THINKING

Design and business once seemed to occupy opposite ends of a spectrum. But in the last ten years, we've seen a growing number of people challenge this assumption. Recent articles on design thinking proliferate—ranging from those that highlight its potential for business to those that warn of its impending decline.

But despite news cycle–driven waxing and waning, the case for adopting a design-thinking approach to business is quite simple and clear. Design thinking helps creators get over unintentional biases and misconceptions to create better, more useful things. Time and again, initiatives falter because they're developed with the host brand, organization, or cause—rather than the target individuals' needs—foremost in mind.

When deep empathy isn't applied to guide decision making, the fear of failure exerts influence over decision processes, and rapid prototyping is rarely used to solicit quick and early feedback. Design thinking offers tools to address these challenges. It helps creators get into other people's heads and hearts, understand their needs, and iteratively test alternative approaches to learn how best to fulfill those needs.

So now we know that design thinking encourages a human-centric orientation, hypothesis testing, and frequent, rapid prototyping. But how do you actually incorporate design thinking into your work?

## ANDY SMITH

*Andy Smith is a principal of Vonavona Ventures, where he advises and bootstraps technical and social ventures with guidance in marketing, customer strategy, and operations. He co-wrote, with his wife, Jennifer Aaker, a professor at Stanford,* The Dragonfly Effect: Quick, Effective, and Powerful Ways To Use Social Media To Drive Social Change. *Follow Andy on Twitter at @kabbenbock and on the Web at DragonflyEffect.com.*

Here are three ways to get started:

### Think human

Focus on your audience rather than making assumptions about them. What are their goals and dreams? How can you help your audience achieve these goals and dreams? What do you want your audience to do? How might they resist? Where are your leverage points that will cause them to act? Don't rush in with a single solution, though! Test some alternatives, and be prepared to return to square one several times.

### Connect with people

Tell stories. Stories are sticky: they bring facts to life and infuse them with context and passion. Physiologically, our brains are hard-wired to process stories. Stories organize and orient complex information for us. Psychologically, we need patterns to help us understand the world. Telling stories also increases the chance that your audience will be able to visualize what you are talking about and thus remember it (humans remember 85 or 90 percent of what we see, but less than 15 percent of what we hear). Salient, meaningful messages, however brief, mobilize communities.

### Turn ripples into waves

Learn from trials. Think critically. Iterate. The right tests—and the subsequent tweaks—can amplify growth. Small details (wording, images, placement of links, etc.) can massively affect your campaign. Use social media tools as a cost-effective way to observe users and refine your approach.

*It is not about how differentiated our stuff is; it's about whether we can make a difference to people.*

While greater success is a welcome and likely outcome of the application of design thinking, the key to understanding it is to realize that it's not just about making a product that will sell more. As Umair Haque writes in The New Capitalist Manifesto, "In the industrial era, firms sought to differentiate products and services. The name of the game was adding perceived value through more elaborate brands, cleverer slogans, or more gripping ads. Difference, in contrast, is not about how differentiated our stuff is, but [about] whether we can make a difference to people, communities, society, and future generations." If all you want is to differentiate yourself, there are a million tips and tricks out there waiting for you. If you want to work more meaningfully, design thinking will help you lead the way.

## WHAT DOES IT TAKE TO DO GREAT WORK?

Based on my own forty years in the world of work, here's what I've found Great Work isn't—and what it is.

It isn't owning a fancy job title. Or having a position at a prestigious institution. It isn't having a big salary. Or a lot of people reporting to you and making you feel important.

For me, great work starts with being part of a great team. Your own work will benefit from being part of a committed, smart, energetic group of people. People you can make common cause with, people you can learn from, people you can fight for—and even fight with. At Fast Company magazine, my simple rule of thumb was, if I hired someone, and then in the morning I tried to avoid walking anywhere near his desk because I didn't want to deal with him, that was a bad hire.

Second, purpose. Great work stems from having a powerful purpose. When I worked for the mayor of Portland, Oregon, our purpose wasn't to win the next election; it was to save Portland from becoming a mini-version of Los Angeles. It was to create America's most livable city. A powerful purpose informs great work.

And third, personal growth and development. It's hard to do great work if you don't feel like you're growing. In fact, one way to know when it's time to change your work is when it becomes routine, when it loses its capacity to surprise and challenge you.

People, purpose, personal growth—when you have all three, you've got the conditions for great work.

If you want to run a simple diagnostic test, here's how to do it.

## ALAN WEBBER

*Alan Webber co-founded and was co-editor of* Fast Company *magazine, having spent years as managing editor and editorial director of the* Harvard Business Review. *He captures much of his wisdom from those experiences in his book,* Rules of Thumb: 52 Truths for Winning at Business Without Losing Your Self. *Follow Alan on Twitter at @alanmwebber and on the Web at RulesOfThumbBook.com.*

*Are you doing something at work that genuinely excites and stimulates you? If not, why not?*

Take a 3 × 5 card. On one side, write down what gets you up in the morning. What are you excited about that awaits you as the day begins? Is it a chance to contribute to a project at work? A colleague you can't wait to work with? Whatever the answer, write it down.

On the other side of the card, write down what keeps you up at night. Is there a concern that you go to bed at night thinking about? A nagging social issue? A career path you wish you could be on? Again, write it down without judging the merits of your answer. Just be truthful.

Then read your answers.

Are you doing something at work that genuinely excites and stimulates you? If not, why not?

Is there something that keeps you up at night that you wish you could be spending more time on? If not, why not?

Use this one simple exercise—and keep the 3 × 5 card—as a device to check in with yourself.

It's a tool to help you do more great work—and avoid getting stuck wasting your time and your life on work you don't really care about and can't possibly do with real greatness!

## A HOPE TO DREAM

On any given day, more than 2 million children in the United States go to sleep without one very important necessity: a bed.

But the implications of not having a warm bed to sleep in are far greater than the mere question of comfort; safety, health, and general living conditions.

The families of these children are trying to get back on their feet. Some come from homeless shelters after having had financial difficulties and don't have the resources to buy furniture. Others are simply struggling. They live in low-income areas and can't afford the cost of a mattress.

The truth of the matter is that the ground or a poorly made mattress is bad for your health. It can lead to significant health problems such as lower back pain and sleep deprivation. In fact, an estimated 70 million Americans suffer from sleep deprivation each year.

But Ashley Sleep believes in a good night's rest.

We believe that a quality night's sleep should be available to everyone, which is precisely why we launched our "A Hope to Dream" program.

Founded in 2010 by Ashley Furniture HomeStore, "A Hope To Dream" seeks to provide thousands of children with a mattress set— an essential part of a good night's sleep. For every mattress sold in enterprise stores, $5 will be donated to the "A Hope To Dream" campaign.

## ASHLEY SLEEP

*Ashley Sleep was developed by Ashley Furniture Industries in 2009 to take advantage of the growing segment of the Specialty Bedding market. Their retail stores contribute several millions of dollars annually to local and national charities. A Hope to Dream is one of the company's many philanthropic efforts.*

*The implications of not having a warm bed to sleep in are far greater than the mere question of comfort; safety, health, and general living conditions.*

Our goal for 2011 is to donate 5,000 mattresses to less fortunate children. What's more, we aim to double that figure in 2012.

Doing the right thing and helping those in need is every bit as important as a good night's sleep. In fact, we believe they go hand in hand. So while Ashley Sleep aims to get high-quality mattresses into the hands of consumers at an affordable price, A Hope to Dream wants no child to ever sleep on a cold floor again.

## ABOUT THIS BOOK

It isn't very often that a book has the power to save a life. Yes, good books can improve lives, shape lives, even change lives. But when was the last time a book literally helped save a life? If you're reading this page, the answer is right now.

The Domino Project in conjunction with Box of Crayons is working with Malaria No More to help end malaria. We're doing this by giving $20 from the purchase of every book to Malaria No More to send a mosquito net to a family in need and to support life-saving work in the fight against malaria.

At its core, *End Malaria* is about doing great work, and at The Domino Project we believe there's no better work than saving a life. Please share this book with your friends, family, and coworkers, and encourage them to join us on our quest.

The sad truth is that every 45 seconds a child dies from Malaria. Thanks to your purchase, we can put some time back on the clock.

## THANK YOU

To Seth Godin and the team at Amazon for not only saying Yes to this project, but also doing this at absolutely no cost, so we can generate an extraordinary amount of money from every sale—thank you.

To the team at The Domino Project for throwing themselves into this project with everything you've got—thank you.

To Scott Case and the team at Malaria No More for sharing their resources and knowledge throughout the production of this book.

To all of the contributors who not only gave us their wisdom, but also graciously allowed me to hound them in their busy lives.

To Workman Publishing, publishers of *Do More Great Work* and early supporters of the project.

To the many people who support me in my life—my wife and business partner Marcella, the team behind Box of Crayons (Ana, Charlotte, Ernest, Kathryn, Robert, Shalon, Sylvana, Tim, and Warren), my Brain Trust—thank you.

And if you've bought a copy of this book, given a copy away, or raised awareness of it—thank you.

Michael Bungay Stanier,
Founder of Box of Crayons

# RESOURCES

## ENDMALARIADAY.COM

## MALARIA TWEETS

You can help us spread the word of this book through Twitter, Facebook, and any of the other social media sites.

We use the hashtag #endmalariaday

Malaria No More tweets as @malarianomore

Tweet to beat malaria. Help us end malaria this #endmalariaday. bit.ly/mAlAriA

Make today #endmalariaday. Tweet to help beat malaria. bit.ly/mAlAriA

Did you know the gin & tonic was invented for malaria? Raise a glass & buy the book to support #endmalariaday. bit.ly/mAlAriA

Every 45 seconds a child dies of malaria. Nets save lives. So can this book #endmalariaday. bit.ly/mAlAriA

By the end of today, 1800 kids will lose their lives. You can help change that. Buy our book and RT #endmalariaday. bit.ly/mAlAriA